THE ULTIMATE
SHEFFIELD UNITED FC
TRIVIA BOOK

A Collection of Amazing Trivia Quizzes
and Fun Facts for Die-Hard Blades Fans!

Ray Walker

Exclusive Free Book
Crazy Sports Stories

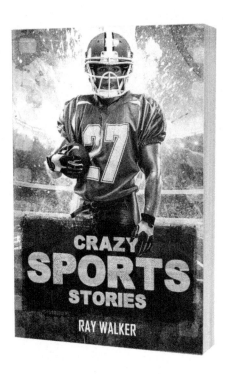

As a thank you for getting a copy of this book I would like to offer you a free copy of my book Crazy Sports Stories which comes packed with interesting stories from your favorite sports such as Football, Hockey, Baseball, Basketball and more.

Grab your free copy over at
RayWalkerMedia.com/Bonus

CONTENTS

INTRODUCTION

The Sheffield United Cricket Club decided to form a soccer team way back in 1889, and that's how one of England's oldest clubs came to be. First nicknamed "The Cutlers" and now known as "The Blades," the team worked its way through the Midland and Northern Leagues to become a founding member of the English Premier League in 1992.

The club is one of just a few to win championships in the top four tiers of the Football League pyramid and has also hoisted the FA Cup more than once. There have also been some disappointments along the way, such as relegations and the failure to qualify for European competition so far.

Still, even as there's so much more for the team to accomplish, its loyal and passionate fans attend Bramall Lane regularly to support their soccer heroes.

Sheffield United may have been demoted from the top-tier a few times over the years, but they always seem to bounce back sooner rather than later.

The club's history is certainly an intriguing and colorful one that deserves to be shared with as many fans as possible.

Blades supporters have had the pleasure of witnessing some of the league's best players and managers work their magic at Bramall Lane throughout the decades, with such unforgettable characters as: J.B. Wostinholm, John Nicholson, Nigel Clough, Chris Wilder, William "Fatty" Foulke, Alan Hodgkinson, Simon Tracey, Paddy Kenny, Paul Stancliffe, Phil Jagielka, Harry Maguire, Tony Currie, Trevor Hockey, Curtis Woodhouse, Paul Devlin, Stephen Quinn, John Fleck, Alan Woodward, Keith Edwards, Tony Agana, Brian Deane, Petr Katchouro, Billy Sharp, David McGoldrick, Ernest Needham, Joe Shaw, Len Badger, Billy Gillespie, and Cec Coldwell.

This latest trivia book has been published to celebrate and remember the history of Sheffield United and to look back at many key moments in the annals of the club. We've gone all the way back to day one and covered the ongoing adventure up to the conclusion of the 2020-21 campaign.

You'll be able to meet the side's most beloved members and learn how each of them left his individual mark on the club.

The Blades' story is presented here in quiz form with 12 unique chapters, each representing a different topic. Each section features 20 challenging quiz questions along with 10 fascinating "Did You Know?" facts. The questions in each quiz are divided into multiple-choice and true-false options, and the answers are presented on a separate page.

This is the ideal way to sharpen your Blades knowledge and challenge yourself on the history of the club. Of course, you'll then be more confident than ever about challenging other Sheffield United and soccer fans to trivia showdowns.

CHAPTER 1:

ORIGINS & HISTORY

QUIZ TIME!

1. What year was Sheffield United FC founded?

    a. 1902

    b. 1899

    c. 1894

    d. 1889

2. The new soccer club was formed out of the existing Sheffield United Cricket Club.

    a. True

    b. False

3. Who was a key founding member of Sheffield United?

    a. William Bailey

    b. J.B. Wostinholm

    c. Charles Clegg

    d. Jonathan Stokes

4. Which club did Sheffield United play its first match against?

a. Sheffield Wednesday

b. Notts Rangers

c. West Bromwich Albion

d. Preston North End

5. What is the club's nickname?

a. "The Blades"

b. "The Ground Breakers"

c. "The Buccaneers"

d. "The Bolts"

6. What was the first league the team joined?

a. The Northern League

b. The Football Alliance

c. The Midlands Counties League

d. The Combination League

7. Sheffield United originally introduced a crest in 1910-11.

a. True

b. False

8. What was the outcome of the side's first match?

a. 1-0 win

b. 2-2 draw

c. 3-0 win

d. 4-1 loss

9. Sheffield United has played its home games at what stadium since the club's inception?

a. Alderson Park

b. Clough Road

c. Bramall Lane

d. Norfolk Park

10. What was the first club Sheffield United faced in the English Football League?

a. Bootle FC

b. Lincoln City FC

c. Ardwick FC

d. Northwich Victoria FC

11. What was the team's original kit color?

a. Powder blue

b. White

c. Amber

d. Red and black stripes

12. Sheffield United was a founding member of the English Premier League.

a. True

b. False

13. What was the outcome of the squad's first Football League match?

a. 5-0 win

b. 2-0 loss

c. 0-0 draw

d. 4-2 win

14. How many games did Sheffield United win in its first domestic league season in 1890-91?

a. 5

b. 10

c. 3

d. 8

15. Who scored the club's first goal in the Premier League?

    a. Brian Deane

    b. Alan Cork

    c. Mitch Ward

    d. Franz Carr

16. Sheffield United was the first professional British soccer club to use the name "United."

    a. True

    b. False

17. Which club did Sheffield United play in its first Premier League match?

    a. Liverpool FC

    b. Middlesbrough FC

    c. Wimbledon FC

    d. Manchester United

18. How many games did the side win in its first Football League season in 1892-93?

    a. 19

    b. 16

    c. 12

    d. 10

19. What was the outcome of Sheffield United's first Premier League match?

    a. 1-0 loss
    b. 1-1 draw
    c. 2-1 win
    d. 3-0 loss

20. The club was promoted in its first Football League season.

    a. True
    b. False

QUIZ ANSWERS

1. D – 1889

2. A – True

3. C – Charles Clegg

4. B – Notts Rangers

5. A – "The Blades"

6. C – The Midlands Counties League

7. B – False

8. D – 4-1 loss

9. C – Bramall Lane

10. B – Lincoln City FC

11. B – White

12. A – True

13. D – 4-2 win

14. D – 8

15. A – Brian Deane

16. A – True

17. D – Manchester United

18. B – 16

19. C – 2-1 win

20. A – True

DID YOU KNOW?

1. Sheffield United Football Club, which goes by the nickname "The Blades," was formed in 1889 and is located in Sheffield, South Yorkshire, England. The club will be playing in the second-tier Championship League in the 2021-22 season. Its home games are played at the Bramall Lane Stadium, which has a seating capacity of just over 32,000 fans. The team is currently owned by Abdullah bin Musa'ad bin Abdulaziz Al Saud of Saudi Arabia, with Yusuf Giansiracusa as the acting chairman.

2. Sheffield United was formed on the evening of March 22, 1889, at 10 Norfolk Row, the offices of Joseph Wostinholm and the Bramall Lane Ground Committee. Present at the meeting were Charles Clegg, chairman of the local football association and Sheffield Wednesday soccer club and president of the local cricket club; David Haigh, and several others. It was decided the new club would be operated by a committee including Haigh, W.F. Beardshaw, and Joseph Tomlinson of the Heeley Football Club. Clegg turned down a role on the committee due to his involvement with the FA but volunteered advice. However, he later became the club's president and chairman.

3. The club was an offshoot of and was named after the local Sheffield United Cricket Club and became the first senior

soccer team in Britain to incorporate the word "United" into its title. The side played in cup competitions in 1889-90, joined the semi-professional Midland League in 1890-91, and entered the semi-pro and amateur Northern League for the 1891-92 campaign. In 1892-93, the club joined the newly formed Second Division in the professional English Football League.

4. In 1892, Sheffield United became the first league club to score 10 goals in a match when they did it against Burslem Port Vale. A year later, the club became the first in the Football League to be promoted to a higher division via a playoff system when they defeated Accrington after finishing the 1892-93 season in second place.

5. The first divisional title for the club came in 1897-98 when it was crowned champions of the Football League's First Division. The same season, the side also became the first winner of the FA Charity Shield match, which was renamed the Community Shield. The team's first FA Cup triumph came in 1898-99.

6. Sheffield United was a founding member of the English Premier League in the inaugural 1992-93 season. The team scored the first goal of the newly created league when Brian Deane struck in a 2-1 home victory over that campaign's eventual champions, Manchester United.

7. Since its formation, Sheffield United has played in the top four tiers of the English Football League and is just one of a few clubs to have won a league championship in all four

tiers. However, most of its history has been spent in the top-tier. For most of the club's history, the team has played in red-and-white striped shirts with black shorts.

8. The club's heyday was the 30 years from 1895 to 1925 when it captured several pieces of silverware. Its darkest days came between 1975 and 1981 after being relegated from the first to the fourth tier of the Football League. The club was demoted to the third tier again in 1988 but was back in the top-flight by 1990 after a 14-year absence.

9. In September 2013, H.R.H. Prince Abdullah bin Musa'ad bin Abdulaziz Al Saud of the royal House of Saud had bought a 50% stake in Sheffield United's parent company, Blades Leisure Ltd. In late 2017, co-owner Kevin McCabe gave Prince Abdullah an option to sell his 50% of the club for £5 million or purchase McCabe's 50% for the same price. Prince Abdullah chose to buy the shares, but McCabe refused to sell them. The matter was then settled in court 20 months later, and Prince Abdullah became the sole owner of the club.

10. During the Premier League era, Sheffield United has been relegated four times, with the most recent coming in 2020-21 after finishing in last place in the league. This also included a stint in the third tier of the league for the first time since 1989. The club has also earned three promotions during the same period and has competed in its divisional playoffs a total of seven times.

CHAPTER 2:

ODDS & ENDS

QUIZ TIME!

1. What was Sheffield United's original nickname?

   a. "The Oaks"

   b. "The Cutlers"

   c. "The Steelers"

   d. "The Bowlers"

2. Bramall Lane is one of the oldest soccer stadiums in the world.

   a. True

   b. False

3. The Steel City Derby is the name of the rivalry between the Blades and which other club?

   a. Leeds United

   b. Sheffield Wednesday

   c. Rotherham United

   d. Barnsley FC

4. How many times has the club been relegated in the Football League as of 2021?

    a. 4

    b. 7

    c. 8

    d. 12

5. Who was the first Sheffield United player to make an appearance for a national team?

    a. Ernest Needham and Alex Forbes

    b. Hugh Morris

    c. Harry Lilley and Michael Whitham

    d. Rab Howell

6. Who is the youngest player to make an appearance for Sheffield United at 16 years and 257 days old?

    a. Diego De Girolamo

    b. Regan Slater

    c. Louis Reed

    d. Antwoine Hackford

7. As of 2021, the Blades have spent 68 seasons in the top-flight of the Football League.

    a. True

    b. False

8. What was the first international tournament Sheffield United participated in?

    a. UEFA Cup

    b. Texaco Cup

c.   Inter-Cities Fairs Cup

d.   Anglo-Italian Cup

9. What is the fewest games the Blades have won in a domestic league season as of 2020-21?

a.   13

b.   11

c.   9

d.   6

10. When was Sheffield United relegated for the first time?

a.   1927-28

b.   1933-34

c.   1951-52

d.   1965-66

11. Who was the first player ever to come on as a substitute for the Blades?

a.   Len Badger

b.   Frank Barlow

c.   Tony Wagstaff

d.   Ken Mallender

12. Sheffield United did not join a league in its first five seasons as a professional club.

a.   True

b.   False

13. Which year did the club introduce the first design of its current crest?

a. 1968

b. 1977

c. 1980

d. 1984

14. The Blades' lowest official attendance in a domestic league match was 4,014 fans watching a match against what club in 1935?

    a. Newcastle United

    b. Port Vale FC

    c. Bradford City FC

    d. Nottingham Forest FC

15. Who was the oldest player to make an appearance for Sheffield United at 39 years and 236 days old?

    a. Stuart McCall

    b. Gary Speed

    c. Phil Jagielka

    d. Jimmy Hagan

16. The first club the Blades faced in an international competition was AS Roma.

    a. True

    b. False

17. In which year was Sheffield United Women FC founded?

    a. 2004

    b. 2002

    c. 1999

    d. 1995

18. What is the fewest points Sheffield United has recorded in a top-flight season as of 2020-21?

    a. 26
    b. 23
    c. 22
    d. 19

19. The lowest official home attendance in all competitions was 3,531 fans in a League Cup match against what club on September 19, 2000?

    a. Colchester United
    b. Wimbledon FC
    c. Bolton Wanderers FC
    d. Northampton Town FC

20. Daniel Jebbison was the youngest player to make an appearance for Sheffield United in the Premier League.

    a. True
    b. False

QUIZ ANSWERS

1. B – "The Cutlers"

2. A – True

3. B – Sheffield Wednesday

4. D – 12

5. C – Harry Lilley and Michael Whitham

6. C – Louis Reed

7. B – False

8. B – Texaco Cup

9. D – 6

10. B – 1933-34

11. C – Tony Wagstaff

12. B – False

13. B – 1977

14. D – Nottingham Forest FC

15. D – Jimmy Hagan

16. B – False

17. B – 2002

18. C – 22

19. A – Colchester United

20. B – False

DID YOU KNOW?

1. The Sheffield United Cricket Club, which helped form the soccer team, was originally formed in 1854 and was the first English sports club to use the word "United" in its name. The soccer club's nickname, "The Blades," came about due to the city's status as a "steel town" and major producer of cutlery. In fact, many fans called the club "The Cutlers" from 1889 to 1912, while Sheffield Wednesday was nicknamed "The Blades." However, Sheffield Wednesday became known as "The Owls" in 1907, and Sheffield United later became known as "The Blades."

2. Bramall Lane, which opened on April 30, 1855, was first used as the home venue of the Yorkshire County Cricket Club from 1855 to 1893. The Sheffield Wednesday soccer club also played its home games there between 1873 and 1884. However, the soccer team moved to a new ground at Olive Grove after a dispute over gate receipts at Bramall Lane. Sheffield United has played its home contests there since the club was formed in 1889.

3. The Bramall Lane venue is considered the oldest major stadium in the world that is still hosting pro soccer games. The stadium was named after the Bramall family, who were file and graver manufacturers. The family owned the Old White House at the corner of Bramall Lane and Cherry Street and then built the Sheaf House pub at the

top of Bramall Lane. The stadium regularly hosted FA Cup semifinals and replays between 1889 and 1938.

4. Sheffield United became the first foreign club to purchase a Chinese team when it bought Chengdu Wuniu in 2006. The club's crest was redesigned in the style of the Sheffield United badge, and the team was renamed the Chengdu Blades. However, the side was dissolved in 2015, five years after Sheffield United had sold its shares. Sheffield United also has operating, business, and exchange of ideas links with Central Coast Mariners of Australia and White Star Woluwé of Belgium. In November 2020, they took over third-tier club Quartz FC of India and renamed it Kerala United FC.

5. The Blades have played in red-and-white striped shirts, black shorts, and red socks at home for most of its history, but started by wearing white shirts and blue shorts. They also played in all white at times during the early years, as well as narrow red stripes in 1890-91. The shirts have featured different collar designs over the years, and white socks have been worn at times. In 1974-75, elements of black were worn on the shirts for several seasons. Sheffield United's home colors were the inspiration for the kit of Irish club Derry City.

6. The first time a crest appeared on Sheffield United's shirts was in 1891-92 when a red crest was featured on the white shirt. However, the crest was gone the following season. The club used the city of Sheffield's coat of arms from

1965 to 1977 when a new crest was used. This crest has been altered slightly a few times.

7. Sheffield United has numerous rivalries, most of them with other Yorkshire-based clubs. The most notable rivalry is with their city neighbors Sheffield Wednesday. Games between the two Sheffield-based clubs are known as the Steel City Derby. Matches against Leeds United are known as the Yorkshire Derby, and the team's other main rivalries are with South Yorkshire clubs Barnsley, Doncaster Rovers, and Rotherham United; those contests are known as South Yorkshire Derbies. West Ham United has also become a rival due to a past transfer saga regarding Carlos Tevez.

8. Like most of the world's soccer clubs, Sheffield United supporters sing a wide variety of songs and chants at home matches. The most famous of these is the "The Greasy Chip Butty Song," sung to the tune of "Annie's Song," which was written and sung by American performer John Denver.

9. A Player of the Year award has been presented by Sheffield United since 1967 to recognize the player who has made the greatest contribution to the club during the season. This award was initially organized and voted on by the team's Official Supporters Club and was presented as an official club award. Voting is now open to a broader section of the club's fan base.

10. Sheffield United operates a women's soccer team that was formerly known as Sheffield United Ladies and is now called Sheffield United Women Football Club (WFC). The team competes in the FA Women's Championship and was originally formed in 2002 as Sheffield United Community Girls and Ladies. The team, which is also nicknamed "The Blades," plays its home matches at Technique Stadium in Chesterfield, which has a capacity of just over 10,500.

CHAPTER 3:

PLAYER OF THE YEAR

QUIZ TIME!

1. Who was the first player to win the Player of the Year award for Sheffield United?

    a. Alan Woodward

    b. Dave Powell

    c. Ken Mallender

    d. Alan Hodgkinson

2. Aaron Ramsdale won both the Player of the Year and the Young Player of the Year award in 2020-21.

    a. True

    b. False

3. Petr Katchouro, the first winner of the Player of the Year award not born in the British Isles, was born in what country?

    a. Lithuania

    b. Estonia

    c. Latvia

    d. Belarus

4. How many times has the Player of the Year award been given to a goalkeeper as of 2021?

   a. 13
   b. 10
   c. 7
   d. 5

5. Who was the first Blades player to win the Player of the Year award in the Premier League era?

   a. Carl Bradshaw
   b. Paul Beesley
   c. Adrian Littlejohn
   d. Tom Cowan

6. How many appearances did Matthew Kilgallon make when he won the Player of the Year award in 2008-09?

   a. 31
   b. 38
   c. 44
   d. 49

7. Alan Woodward was the first player to win the Player of the Year award four times.

   a. True
   b. False

8. Who was the winner of the club's Young Player of the Year award in 2011-12?

   a. Matt Harriott
   b. George Long

c. Harry Maguire

d. John Egan

9. How many goals did Keith Edwards score in the 1983-84 season when he took home the Player of the Year award?

   a. 28

   b. 33

   c. 39

   d. 41

10. The first non-English-born winner of the Player of the Year award hailed from which country?

    a. Northern Ireland

    b. Wales

    c. Scotland

    d. Ireland

11. How many appearances did Ché Adams make in 2015-16 when he won the Young Player of the Year award?

    a. 37

    b. 45

    c. 34

    d. 41

12. Dave Powell played just 28 games in 1968-69 when he was named Player of the Year.

    a. True

    b. False

13. Who was the first player to win the club's Young Player of the Year award while competing in the Premier League?

a. Dean Henderson

b. Oliver McBurnie

c. Lys Mousset

d. Callum Robinson

14. How many times has a defender won the Player of the Year award?

    a. 8

    b. 11

    c. 14

    d. 18

15. Scottish international Paul Devlin, the winner of the Player of the Year award in 1999-2000, was born in what country?

    a. England

    b. Australia

    c. New Zealand

    d. Canada

16. In 2016-17, the Player of the Year award was shared between John Fleck and Billy Sharp.

    a. True

    b. False

17. Who won the Young Player of the Year award in 2014-15?

    a. Ben Whiteman

    b. Harrison McGahey

    c. Louis Reed

    d. Dominick Calvert-Lewin

18. How many goals did Billy Sharp score to win the 2015-16 Player of the Year award?

    a. 25
    b. 21
    c. 17
    d. 11

19. How many times did Phil Jagielka win the Player of the Year award?

    a. 5
    b. 3
    c. 1
    d. 0

20. Tony Agana scored 29 goals in 58 appearances to win the Player of the Season award in 1988-89.

    a. True
    b. False

QUIZ ANSWERS

1. D – Alan Hodgkinson

2. A – True

3. D – Belarus

4. C – 7

5. B – Paul Beesley

6. D – 49

7. A – True

8. C – Harry Maguire

9. C – 39

10. B – Wales

11. D – 41

12. A – True

13. A – Dean Henderson

14. D – 18

15. A – England

16. A – True

17. C – Louis Reed

18. B – 21

19. B – 3

20. A – True

DID YOU KNOW?

1. Goalkeepers who have been voted the Sheffield United Player of the Year are: 1966-67, Alan Hodgkinson; 1974-75, Jim Brown; 1989-90, Simon Tracey; 1991-92, Simon Tracey; 1995-96, Alan Kelly; 2002-03, Paddy Kenny; 2020-21, Aaron Ramsdale.

2. Defenders who have taken home the club's Player of the Year award are: 1967-68, Ken Mallender; 1968-69, Dave Powell; 1972-73, Ted Hemsley; 1985-86, Paul Stancliffe; 1987-88, Paul Stancliffe; 1992-93, Paul Beesley; 1993-94, Carl Bradshaw; 1997-98, Nicky Marker; 2000-01, Shaun Murphy; 2003-04, Chris Morgan; 2004-05, Phil Jagielka; 2005-06, Phil Jagielka; 2006-07; Phil Jagielka; 2008-09, Matthew Kilgallon; 2011-12, Harry Maguire; 2012-13, Harry Maguire; 2013-14, Harry Maguire; 2019-20, Chris Basham.

3. Sheffield United midfielders who have been voted Player of the Year are: 1970-71, Tony Currie; 1971-72, Trevor Hockey; 1981-82, Mike Trusson; 1982-83, Mike Trusson; 1984-85, Glenn Cockerill; 1986-87, Peter Beagrie; 1994-95, Kevin Gage; 1998-99, Curtis Woodhouse; 1999-2000, Paul Devlin; 2001-02, Michael Brown; 2009-10, Nick Montgomery; 2010-11, Stephen Quinn; 2014-15, Jamie Murphy; 2016-17, John Fleck; 2017-18, John Fleck.

4. Forwards who have won the side's Player of the Year award are: 1969-70, Alan Woodward; 1973-74, Alan Woodward; 1975-76, Alan Woodward; 1976-77, Keith Edwards; 1977-78, Alan Woodward; 1978-79, Tony Kenworthy; 1979-80, Tony Kenworthy; 1980-81, Bob Hatton; 1983-84, Keith Edwards; 1988-89, Tony Agana; 1990-91, Brian Deane; 1996-97, Petr Katchouro; 2007-08, James Beattie; 2015-16, Billy Sharp; 2016-17, Billy Sharp; 2018-19, David McGoldrick.

5. Those who have won the Player of the Year award more than once, as of the conclusion of the 2020-21 season, are: Alan Woodward, four times, in 1969-70, 1973-74, 1975-76, and 1977-78; Phil Jagielka, three times, in 2004-05, 2005-06, and 2006-07; Harry Maguire, three times, in 2011-12, 2012-13, and 2013-14; Tony Kenworthy, twice, in 1978-1979 and 1979-1980; Mike Trusson, twice, in 1981-82 and 1982-83; Keith Edwards, twice, in 1976-77 and 1983-84; Paul Stancliffe, twice, in 1985-86 and 1987-88; Simon Tracey, twice, in 1989-90 and 1991-92; Billy Sharp, twice, in 2015-16 and 2016-17; John Flecks, twice, in 2016-17 and 2017-18.

6. Goalkeepers have won the award seven times, defenders have won it 18 times, midfielders have won it 15 times, and forwards have won it 16 times. The award was shared in 2016-17 by midfielder John Fleck and forward Billy Sharp.

7. Alan Hodgkinson was the first goalkeeper and player to win the inaugural award, in 1966-67. Ken Mallender was

the first defender to win the trophy, in 1967-68. Alan Woodward was the first forward to win it, in 1969-70, and the first midfielder to win it was Tony Currie, in 1970-71.

8. Dave Powell of Wales was the first non-English winner of the Player of the Year award in 1968-69. Alan Woodward was the first player to win the trophy twice, three times, and four times. However, Tony Kenworthy was the first to win it in consecutive seasons. Phil Jagielka then became the first player to win the award for three successive seasons.

9. The winner of the Player of the Year award has hailed from Australia, Belarus, the Republic of Ireland, and Wales once each, while three winners were born in Scotland. The rest hailed from England. Trevor Hockey was born in England and played internationally for Wales. Paul Devlin and Nick Montgomery were born in England but represented Scotland. David McGoldrick, Alan Kelly Jr., and Paddy Kenny were born in England and played for the Republic of Ireland.

10. Since 2011-12, the club has also handed out a Young Player of the Year trophy. The winners have been: 2011-12, Harry Maguire (defender); 2012-13, George Long (goalkeeper); 2013-14, Connor Dimaio (midfielder); 2014-15, Louis Reed (midfielder); 2015-16, Ché Adams (forward); 2016-17, David Brooks (midfielder); 2017-18, David Brooks (midfielder); 2018-19, Dean Henderson (goalkeeper); 2019-20, Dean Henderson (goalkeeper);

2020-21, Aaron Ramsdale (goalkeeper). Ramsdale also won the Player of the Year award for 2020-21. David Brooks was born in England and plays internationally with Wales. Connor Dimaio was born in England and plays internationally for the Republic of Ireland. Ché Adams was born in England and plays internationally with Scotland. The rest of the winners hail from England.

CHAPTER 4:

AMAZING MANAGERS

QUIZ TIME!

1. Who was recognized as Sheffield United's first official secretary manager?

    a. J.B. Wostinholm

    b. Teddy Davison

    c. Reg Freeman

    d. John Nicholson

2. The Blades were managed by a committee until 1940.

    a. True

    b. False

3. Ken Furphy left what club to manage Sheffield United?

    a. Ipswich Town FC

    b. Everton FC

    c. Blackburn Rovers

    d. Watford FC

4. How many managers born in North America have been appointed by Sheffield United as of 2021?

a. 0

b. 1

c. 2

d. 3

5. Who was Sheffield United's first manager in the Premier League?

   a. Ian Porterfield

   b. Billy McEwan

   c. Dave Bassett

   d. Howard Kendall

6. Who replaced Neil Warnock as manager in May 2007?

   a. Bryan Robson

   b. Kevin Blackwell

   c. Gary Speed

   d. Micky Adams

7. Slaviša Jokanović is the Blades' first manager born outside the British Isles.

   a. True

   b. False

8. How many competitive games did Kevin Blackwell win while managing Sheffield United?

   a. 87

   b. 60

   c. 53

   d. 45

9. Who helped the club to promotion to the Premier League in the 2005-06 season?

  a. Neil Warnock

  b. Kevin Blackwell

  c. Bryan Robson

  d. Russell Slade

10. Danny Wilson left what club to become manager of the Blades?

  a. Luton Town FC

  b. Chesterfield FC

  c. Hull City FC

  d. Swindon Town FC

11. Which manager served for 32 years and 11 months?

  a. Cec Coldwell

  b. John Harris

  c. J.B. Wostinholm

  d. John Nicholson

12. Arthur Rowley managed the Blades for only six games before being replaced by John Harris.

  a. True

  b. False

13. Neil Warnock left Sheffield United to manage what team?

  a. Bournemouth AFC

  b. Southampton FC

  c. Crystal Palace FC

  d. Plymouth Argyle FC

14. Who did Slaviša Jokanović replace as manager?

    a. Nigel Adkins
    b. Chris Wilder
    c. Nigel Clough
    d. Chris Morgan

15. How many competitive matches did Nigel Clough manage with Sheffield United?

    a. 96
    b. 104
    c. 119
    d. 130

16. Archie Clark was the first manager of the Blades who was not born in Great Britain.

    a. True
    b. False

17. Ian Porterfield joined Sheffield United from which outfit?

    a. Rotherham United
    b. Chelsea FC
    c. Reading FC
    d. Celtic FC

18. For which season did Chris Wilder win the LMA Manager of the Year award?

    a. 2019-20
    b. 2018-19
    c. 2016-17
    d. 2014-15

19. How many competitive matches did John Harris win with the Blades?

    a. 198
    b. 151
    c. 200
    d. 174

20. As of 2021, seven different Sheffield United managers have won a League Managers Association award.

    a. True
    b. False

QUIZ ANSWERS

1. A – J.B. Wostinholm

2. B – False

3. C – Blackburn Rovers

4. A – 0

5. C – Dave Bassett

6. A – Bryan Robson

7. A – True

8. C – 53

9. A – Neil Warnock

10. D – Swindon Town FC

11. D – John Nicholson

12. B – False

13. C – Crystal Palace FC

14. B – Chris Wilder

15. B – 104

16. B – False

17. A – Rotherham United

18. B – 2018-19

19. D – 174

20. B – False

DID YOU KNOW?

1. When the club was formed in 1889, it was coached by a trainer, while a football committee selected the team and decided upon tactics, similar to the system used by the Sheffield United Cricket Club. Cec Coldwell, Russell Slade, and Chris Morgan each had two stints as caretaker manager of the club. Coldwell's spells came in 1975 and from September 1977 to January 1978. Slade took over for two games in March 1998 and two more matches in late November and early December the following year. Morgan took over twice in 2013. John Harris had two stints as full-time boss, from April 1959 to July 1968 and from August 1969 to December 1973.

2. Joseph "J.B." Wostinholm was the first person to be placed in charge of the club's day-to-day affairs and was officially given the title of secretary but is widely regarded to be the side's first manager. He held his position from 1889 to 1899, winning the First Division title in 1897-98. Wostinholm was also the secretary of the Yorkshire County Cricket Club from 1864 to 1902.

3. When J.B. Wostinholm left the Blades, he was replaced by John Nicholson, who led the team to four FA Cup titles and an FA Cup runner-up medal and held the job until passing away in 1932. He was also officially known as the club secretary but ran the team on a day-to-day basis and

dealt with transfers. The team selection was still handled by a committee, though. Nicholson died in April 1932 at the age of 68 after being hit by a truck outside of Sheffield Midland Station on his way to join the team on a trip to play Aston Villa.

4. Between 2010 and 2011, Sheffield United went through several different managers. Kevin Blackwell held the job from February 2008 to August 2010. He was replaced by Gary Speed from August to December 14, 2010, when John Carver took over for the last two weeks of December. Carver was then replaced by Micky Adams from December 30, 2010, to May 10, 2011, when Danny Wilson was appointed manager in late May 2011. The club was relegated from the second-tier Championship League following the 2010-11 season.

5. Nigel Clough, a former English international player and the son of famous soccer manager Brian Clough, left Derby County to take over as Sheffield United manager in October 2013. He was named League One's Manager of the Month for February 2014 and reached the FA Cup semifinals against Hull City the following season. Clough was named the FA Cup Manager of the Season by the League Managers Association for the team's cup run as a third-tier team. Clough also led the side to the League Cup semifinals in 2014-15, but the club parted company with him on May 25, 2015, and he returned to Burton Albion for a second spell as manager, while Nigel Adkins took over at Bramall Lane.

6. Former Sheffield United ball boy and defender Chris Wilder was appointed the club's boss on May 12, 2016, to take over from Nigel Adkins. In his first season in charge, he took the Blades back to the second tier by winning League One as the side finished the campaign with a club-record 100 points, and he was named the LMA League One Manager of the Year. Wilder earned his second promotion in three seasons when the team finished as the Championship League runner-up in 2018-19 to reach the Premier League. This achievement also saw him win the LMA Manager of the Year award. Wilder left the Blades by mutual consent on March 13, 2021, when the team was in last place in the Premier League with 14 points from 28 games.

7. All of the club's managers have been English other than John Harris, Ian Porterfield, Billy McEwan, and David Weir, who were Scottish, and Gary Speed, who was Welsh. Danny Wilson was born in Wigan, England, but played international soccer with Northern Ireland. Wilson is also one of two former Sheffield United managers who held the same position with city rivals Sheffield Wednesday; Steve Bruce is the other. Wilson was Wednesday's boss in 1998 and also played for the club in the early 1990s. Bruce began his managerial career with the Blades as a player-manager in 1998 and was appointed Wednesday's boss in 2019.

8. The first and only Sheffield United manager to hail from outside of Great Britain as of June 2021 was Slaviša Jokanović of Serbia. He was hired by the Blades on May

27, 2021, to take over the position full-time from Chris Wilder. When Wilder left on March 13, he was replaced in the interim by Paul Heckingbottom. Jokanović is a former Yugoslavian international midfielder who previously managed clubs in Serbia, Thailand, Bulgaria, Spain, Israel, and Qatar. He also managed in England, with Watford and Fulham.

9. The longest-serving Sheffield United managers were: John Nicholson, 32 years, 11 months (1899-1932); Teddy Davison, 20 years (1932-52); J.B Wostinholm, 10 years, two months (1889-99); John Harris, 9 years, three months (1959-68); Dave Basset, seven years, 11 months (1988-95); Neil Warnock, seven years, six months (1999-2007); Chris Wilder, four years, 11 months (2016-21); Ian Porterfield, four years, nine months (1981-86).

10. In winning percentage for managers with at least 100 games in charge, the top 10 are: Danny Wilson, 51.89%; Nigel Clough, 47.12%; Chris Wilder, 46.7%; John Harris, 44.68%; J.B. Wostinholm, 44.21%; Ian Porterfield, 43.36%; Neil Warnock, 42.53%; Kevin Blackwell, 42.4%; Teddy Davison, 41.89%; John Harris, 41.04%.

CHAPTER 5:

GOALTENDING GREATS

QUIZ TIME!

1. Who made the most appearances in all competitions for the Blades?

   a. Jack Smith
   b. Alan Hodgkinson
   c. William Foulke
   d. Simon Tracey

2. Sheffield United had five different keepers make at least one appearance in the 2009-10 domestic league.

   a. True
   b. False

3. How many clean sheets did Paddy Kenny keep in the 2009-09 domestic Championship League?

   a. 20
   b. 17
   c. 22
   d. 13

4. Which club loaned Dean Henderson to the Blades?

    a. Manchester City FC
    b. Aberdeen FC
    c. Manchester United
    d. Portsmouth FC

5. Who played in Sheffield United's first Premier League match?

    a. Mel Rees
    b. Phil Kite
    c. Alan Kelly
    d. Simon Tracey

6. Justin Haber was capped nine times by what national team while playing for Sheffield United?

    a. Italy
    b. Malta
    c. Albania
    d. Monaco

7. Alan Kelly Jr. was capped 22 times by the English men's national team while playing for the Blades.

    a. True
    b. False

8. How many consecutive league appearances did Jack Smith once make for Sheffield United?

    a. 123
    b. 203

c. 245

d. 502

9. Paddy Kenny left Sheffield United to join what club?

   a. Leicester City FC

   b. Liverpool FC

   c. Bury FC

   d. Queens Park Rangers

10. What player kept 11 clean sheets in the 2009-10 Championship League?

    a. Steve Simonsen

    b. Mark Bunn

    c. Richard Wright

    d. Carl Ikeme

11. How many clean sheets did Mark Howard keep in the 2013-14 League One campaign?

    a. 15

    b. 12

    c. 9

    d. 5

12. Alan Hodgkinson played his entire professional career with Sheffield United.

    a. True

    b. False

13. How many appearances did Steve Simonsen make for the club in all competitions?

a. 67

b. 108

c. 383

d. 299

14. What was William Foulke's nickname?

    a. "The Boulder"

    b. "Freak"

    c. "Giraffe"

    d. "Fatty"

15. Who backed up Paddy Kenny in 16 games in the 2003-04 domestic league?

    a. Ian Bennett

    b. Phil Barnes

    c. Alan Fettis

    d. Paul Gerrard

16. Mihkel Aksalu was capped 10 times by the Estonian men's national team while playing with the Blades.

    a. True

    b. False

17. Who appeared in 43 games in the 2016-17 domestic league?

    a. Simon Moore

    b. Mark Howard

    c. Iain Turner

    d. George Long

18. Who recorded 17 clean sheets in the 2011-12 League One season?

    a. Ian Bennett
    b. George Long
    c. Steve Simonsen
    d. Mark Howard

19. How many appearances did Alan Hodgkinson make in all competitions with the squad?

    a. 591
    b. 623
    c. 675
    d. 707

20. Ian Bennett played in all 38 games of the 2006-07 Premier League.

    a. True
    b. False

QUIZ ANSWERS

1. B – Alan Hodgkinson

2. A – True

3. A – 20

4. C – Manchester United

5. D – Simon Tracey

6. B – Malta

7. A – True

8. B – 203

9. D – Queens Park Rangers

10. B – Mark Bunn

11. B – 12

12. A – True

13. B – 108

14. D – "Fatty"

15. D – Paul Gerrard

16. B – False

17. A – Simon Moore

18. C – Steve Simonsen

19. C – 675

20. B – False

DID YOU KNOW?

1. One of the club's first goalkeepers was William "Fatty" Foulke, who was spotted by Sheffield United while playing for village club Blackwell in a Derbyshire Cup match. He joined the Blades in 1894 and remained a fixture between the posts for the next 11 seasons. He helped the team capture the First Division title in 1897-98 and the 1898-99 and 1901-02 FA Cups. He also kept goal in the 1900-01 final when the side finished as runner-up and as the First Division runner-up in 1896-97 and 1899-1900. After approximately 350 games, he joined Chelsea in May 1905 for a reported £50 fee. Foulke reportedly stood 6 feet 4 inches tall and weighed about 300 pounds. He was also a top-class cricket player, and his nephew, Jim Simmons, won the 1915 FA Cup with Sheffield United. Foulke passed away in May 1916 at 42 years of age.

2. Joining First Division Sheffield United from Castleford Town in April 1913 was Harold Gough. He played in the 1913-14 FA Cup semifinal matches against eventual winners Burnley, with the Blades drawing 0-0 and then losing the replay 1-0. However, Gough won the FA Cup the following season by shutting out Chelsea 3-0. Football League action was then paused due to World War I, and he returned to the club for the 1919-20 campaign as the team's regular keeper. Gough appeared in over 250 games

for the Blades over an 11-year span and rejoined Castleford Town in 1924.

3. Jack Alderson began his career with his local club Crook Juniors in 1909 and played with several sides before joining First Division Newcastle United in January 1913. The First World War interrupted his career, and he signed with Southern League club Crystal Palace in 1919 when the conflict ended. The Southern League joined the newly formed Third Division of the Football League in 1920-21. Sheffield United needed a replacement keeper for Charles Sutcliffe and signed Alderson at the age of 34 in 1925. He helped the team reach the 1927-28 FA Cup semifinals. He played over 130 games with the club before joining Exeter City in May 1929, and it was reported that he saved 11 of the 12 penalty kicks he faced in his career.

4. Playing nearly 400 games with Sheffield United was John "Jack" Smith, who signed with the club in 1930 after playing a couple of trial games in the Central League. The popular keeper earned the nickname "Smiler" and once played 203 straight league games for the team between 1935 and 1949, with the streak starting before and ending after World War II. He was with the Blades for 19 years; his final appearance with the squad was in May 1949. Smith's teams were relegated from the First Division in 1933-34 and 1948-49, while earning promotion as runner-up in the second tier in 1938-39.

5. The first Blades keeper and player to be named Player of the Year was Alan Hodgkinson, who took the inaugural

honor for the 1966-67 season. The 5-foot-9-inch English international joined the team in 1953 to kick off his pro career and played with the side 675 times to set a club appearance record for keepers. He debuted in 1954 as a backup to Ted Burgin and became a regular starter in 1957. He was on promotion-winning teams in 1960-61 and 1970-71. Hodgkinson remained with the club until 1971 when John Hope took over as the first-choice keeper. He was in the England squad for the 1958 and 1962 World Cups but didn't play any of the games and later became one of the world's first full-time goalkeeping coaches.

6. Jim Brown of Scotland began his pro career at Albion Rovers, making his debut as a 16-year-old in 1968. He arrived at Bramall Lane from Chesterfield on the final day of the transfer window in the 1973-74 season and went on to play more than 200 games with the team. Brown won the team's Player of the Year award for 1974-75 and left the club to play in America in 1979. He earned one international cap for Scotland after representing his homeland five times at the under-23 level.

7. Arriving at Sheffield United from Wimbledon in 1988 was Simon Tracey for a reported fee of £7,500. He helped the side earn consecutive promotions from the Third and Second Divisions, respectively, in 1988-89 and 1989-90 by finishing as runner-up both seasons. He was also named the squad's Player of the Year for his play in 1989-90 and 1991-92. His playing time was reduced due to injuries and the arrival of Alan Kelly Jr. in 1992, and he was sent on

loan to several clubs, including Manchester City, Norwich City, Nottingham Forest, and Wimbledon. Tracey again played regularly for the Blades in the late 1990s and early 2000s and had appeared in more than 380 games before hanging up his boots and gloves in 2003 due to injury.

8. English-born Republic of Ireland international Paddy Kenny initially joined Sheffield United on loan from Bury FC as cover for the injured Simon Tracey in August 2002, and three months later, the loan was made permanent. He helped the side reach the 2002-03 Division One playoff final and was named the club's Player of the Year as it also reached the semifinals of the FA Cup and League Cup. Kenny played every minute of the 2005-06 season when the Blades were promoted to the Premier League as Championship League runners-up, but they were relegated on the final day of the 2006-07 campaign. He reached the Championship League playoff final in 2008-09 but later tested positive for a banned substance found in cough medicine. In September 2009, he was banned for nine months and joined Queens Park Rangers in June 2010 after more than 300 games with the Blades. Kenny also shared the Football League Championship Golden Glove award in 2008-09.

9. English-born Republic of Ireland international Alan Kelly Jr. followed in his father's goalkeeping footsteps and began his career with hometown club Preston North End. He joined the Blades in July 1992 for a reported £150,000 fee and remained at Bramall Lane until joining Blackburn

Rovers in 1999. He was named Sheffield United's Player of the Year for 1995-96 and helped the side reach the semifinals of the 1997-98 FA Cup. Kelly was also named to the First Division PFA Team of the Year in 1995-96 and 1996-97 and played over 250 games with the club.

10. English international Dean Henderson spent his youth career with Manchester United and signed his first pro contract with the club in 2015. He was loaned to Stockport County, Grimsby Town, and Shrewsbury Town before arriving at Bramall Lane on loan in June 2018. He helped the side earn promotion to the Premier League by finishing as second-tier runner-up in 2018-19 when Henderson won the Championship League's Golden Glove award after posting 20 clean sheets and being voted the Blades' Young Player of the Year. Henderson signed a new contract with Man United in July 2019 and returned to Sheffield United on loan. He played 40 times in 2019-20 and was then recalled by Man United after 86 appearances with the Blades.

CHAPTER 6:

DARING DEFENDERS

QUIZ TIME!

1. Who played the most career games with the Blades in all competitions?

    a. Len Badger

    b. Graham Shaw

    c. Joe Shaw

    d. Ernest Needham

2. Greg Halford led the Blades with eight assists in the 2008-09 domestic league.

    a. True

    b. False

3. Who played in 39 games in the 1992-93 Premier League?

    a. Carl Bradshaw

    b. Paul Beesley

    c. Brian Gayle

    d. Tom Cowan

4. How many goals did Enda Stevens score in the 2019-20 Premier League?

    a. 1
    b. 5
    c. 2
    d. 7

5. Roger Nilsen was capped 15 times by which men's national team while playing for Sheffield United?

    a. Finland
    b. Denmark
    c. Norway
    d. Sweden

6. Which club did Eddie Colquhoun leave to join Sheffield United?

    a. Swansea City FC
    b. Hull City FC
    c. Sunderland AFC
    d. West Bromwich Albion

7. Joe Shaw played his entire professional career with the Blades.

    a. True
    b. False

8. How many appearances did Len Badger make for Sheffield United in all competitions?

    a. 588
    b. 541

c. 510

d. 435

9. Who made 56 appearances in all competitions in 2011-12?

   a. Matthew Lowton

   b. Lecsinel Jean-François

   c. Harry Maguire

   d. Neill Collins

10. Ted Hemsley arrived at Bramall Lane from which team?

    a. Watford FC

    b. Torquay United

    c. Bolton Wanderers

    d. Shrewsbury Town FC

11. How many goals did Matt Done score in all competitions in the 2015-16 domestic league?

    a. 3

    b. 7

    c. 5

    d. 2

12. Jack O'Connell was shown 13 yellow cards in the 2017-18 domestic league.

    a. True

    b. False

13. How many appearances did Harry Maguire make in all competitions for the team?

    a. 43

    b. 78

c. 166

d. 244

14. Who made 43 appearances in the 2002-03 domestic league?

a. Phil Jagielka

b. Shaun Murphy

c. Robert Page

d. Rob Kozluk

15. What player was shown 11 yellow cards in all competitions in 2014-15?

a. Ben Davies

b. Jay McEveley

c. Craig Alcock

d. Chris Basham

16. Leigh Bromby was capped by the English men's national team 16 times while playing for Sheffield United.

a. True

b. False

17. From which club did Chris Morgan join Sheffield United?

a. Preston North End

b. West Bromwich Albion

c. Barnsley FC

d. Crystal Palace FC

18. How many career games did Joe Shaw play for the Blades?

a. 714

b. 686

c. 625

d. 594

19. Which player scored three goals in the 2007-08 Championship League season?

   a. Matthew Kilgallon

   b. Chris Armstrong

   c. Gary Cahill

   d. Chris Morgan

20. Rob Page was capped 41 times by the Welsh men's national team.

   a. True

   b. False

QUIZ ANSWERS

1. C – Joe Shaw

2. A – True

3. B – Paul Beesley

4. C – 2

5. C – Norway

6. D – West Bromwich Albion

7. A – True

8. B – 541

9. C – Harry Maguire

10. D – Shrewsbury Town FC

11. B – 7

12. B – False

13. C – 166

14. B – Shaun Murphy

15. D – Chris Basham

16. B – False

17. C – Barnsley FC

18. A – 714

19. B – Chris Armstrong

20. A – True

DID YOU KNOW?

1. Although he was just 5 feet 5 inches tall, Sheffield-born Rabbi "Rab" Howell carved out a fine career for himself with the Blades. He began his career with local junior club Ecclesfield and Rotherham Swifts before signing with the newly formed Sheffield United club in March 1890. He started as a striker but soon converted to a defender. He helped the team win promotion to the First Division in its inaugural Football League campaign in 1892-93 and won a First Division winners' medal in 1897-98. Howell scored once in two outings for England and, in his final season with Sheffield United, was accused of trying to throw a game after scoring two own-goals against Sunderland. He wasn't charged by the Football Association but was soon sold to Liverpool in 1898, playing over 200 games for the club.

2. Bernard Wilkinson started his soccer career with Thorpe Hesley Parish Church in 1895 and then left Thorpe Hesley in 1899 to join Sheffield United. He helped the side finish as the First Division runner-up in 1899-1900 and winner of the 1901-02 FA Cup, making his one and only England appearance in April 1904. Wilkinson spent 14 seasons with the Blades and served as club captain for a spell. He played his final match for the team and joined Rotherham Town in April 1913 after notching 14 goals in 396 appearances.

Wilkinson was also a fine cricket player. His brother William Wilkinson played seven seasons with Sheffield United between 1901 and 1908 and was also a successful cricket player.

3. The all-time appearance leader for Sheffield United is Joe Shaw at 714 games during his career at Bramall Lane from 1945 to 1966. This total includes 632 league outings and 53 FA Cup ties, which are also club records. Shaw joined the team from Upton Colliery as an inside-forward and later converted into a defender/midfielder. He played for the side in the Football League North during World War II in 1944-45 when he was just over 16 years old and made his league debut in August 1948. He enjoyed three stints as team captain. After hanging up his boots in 1966, he became a soccer manager. He was relegated with the team twice and also promoted twice by winning the 1952-53 Second Division and finishing as runner-up in 1960-61. In 2010, a statue of Shaw was erected at Bramall Lane to commemorate his service to the club.

4. Hometown defender Fred Furniss shone as a youngster when playing soccer for both Sheffield and Yorkshire Boys. He debuted with the Blades as an amateur in the middle of an air raid in a 1941 away game with Everton. He went on to play 433 games and score 18 goals with the club while playing wartime and Football League soccer. The right-back became a first-team regular in 1943 and held his position until 1954. He scored on 15 of his 17 penalty kicks and helped the side win the Wartime

League North Championship in 1945-46 and the Second Division Title in 1952-53. He joined Chesterfield as a player-coach in 1955 and played local league soccer well into his 50s.

5. Born in Sheffield, Graham Shaw played with amateur side Oaks Fold and Sheffield Schoolboys before signing a pro contract with Sheffield United as a 17-year-old in 1951. He went on to make nearly 500 appearances with the club and played five times with England until joining Doncaster Rovers in 1967. He helped the Blades win the Second Division title in 1952-53 and finish as Second Division runners-up in 1960-61 after being relegated in 1955-56. Shaw's younger brother Bernard Shaw also played with Sheffield United as well as Wolverhampton Wanderers and Sheffield Wednesday.

6. George "Cec" Coldwell played his entire pro career for hometown Sheffield United from 1951 to 1968, helping the team win the Second Division in 1952-53 and finishing as runner-up in 1960-61 after being relegated five years earlier. The right-back was acquired from local club Norton Woodseats for a reported fee of £100, and he made his debut in April 1952. He developed fine full-back partnerships with Cliff Mason and Graham Shaw and wore the captain's armband for a spell. Coldwell played in nearly 500 games with the team and contributed a pair of goals. He became a coach for the club and also had two stints as caretaker manager, in 1975 and 1977-78.

7. Former skipper Len Badger represented both Sheffield Boys and England Schoolboys as a youngster and made his senior Sheffield United debut in May 1962 on a tour of America. He was capped at the under-18 and under-23 level by England. In 1966, Badger became the youngest league captain in the history of the Blades and wore the armband until passing it to Eddie Colquhoun in 1968. He helped his hometown team earn promotion by finishing as the Second Division runner-up in 1970-71 after being relegated in 1967-68. He played 541 times for the club and notched eight goals before joining Chesterfield in 1976. After hanging up his boots, Badger later became a match day host at Bramall Lane.

8. Scottish international Edmund "Eddie" Colquhoun joined the club in 1968 from West Bromwich Albion just after the Blades had been relegated to the second tier. He was known for his leadership and hard-tackling abilities and was quickly appointed team captain. He helped the team earn promotion back to the top-tier by finishing as the Second Division runner-up in 1970-71. Colquhoun appeared in more than 400 games for the club and contributed over 20 goals before leaving to play in America in 1978.

9. Central defender Paul Stancliffe was born in Sheffield but kicked off his career with Rotherham United. He played nearly 300 games with the club over seven years before joining Sheffield United in 1983. Stancliffe wore the captain's armband for much of his career with the Blades

and played over 300 matches before joining Wolverhampton Wanderers in 1990. He led Sheffield United to two successive promotions from the Third Division to the First Division, in 1988-89 and 1989-90, and was voted the team's Player of the Year for 1985-86 and 1987-88.

10. Leaving Third Division Aldershot for newly promoted Sheffield United in July 1989 was David Barnes when he was acquired for a reported £50,000 fee. He helped the Blades reach the First Division in his first season as the side finished the year as second-tier runner-up. Barnes was with the team during the inaugural Premier League campaign in 1992-93, but, after his playing time dipped, he left for Watford in January 1994 for a reported £50,000. Barnes played 107 games with Sheffield United over four and a half years and scored one goal.

CHAPTER 7:

MAESTROS OF THE MIDFIELD

QUIZ TIME!

1. Which player made the most appearances for the squad in all competitions?

    a. Michael Tonge

    b. Nick Montgomery

    c. Tony Kenworthy

    d. Tommy Sampy

2. Mick Speight was capped 24 times by the English men's national team.

    a. True

    b. False

3. Who appeared in 44 games in the 2009-10 Championship League?

    a. James Harper

    b. Lee Williamson

    c. Glenn Little

    d. Stephen Quinn

4. Who scored eight goals in the 1992-93 Premier League season?

    a. Glyn Hodges
    b. Dane Whitehouse
    c. Adrian Littlejohn
    d. Ian Bryson

5. How many goals did Jose Baxter score in all competitions in 2014-15?

    a. 6
    b. 8
    c. 13
    d. 16

6. Tony Kenworthy left the Blades to join what club?

    a. Mansfield Town FC
    b. Hull City FC
    c. Grantham Town FC
    d. Queens Park Rangers

7. Oliver Norwood was shown 11 yellow cards in the 2018-19 domestic league.

    a. True
    b. False

8. How many appearances did Chris Armstrong make in all competitions with the club?

    a. 51
    b. 105

c. 360

d. 403

9. Keith Gillespie was capped 15 times by which men's national team while playing for Sheffield United?

    a. USA

    b. Scotland

    c. Northern Ireland

    d. Canada

10. Who scored six goals in all competitions in 2016-17?

    a. Stefan Scougall

    b. Mark Duffy

    c. John Fleck

    d. Paul Coutts

11. How many goals did Lee Williamson score in the 2011-12 League One season?

    a. 7

    b. 9

    c. 12

    d. 15

12. Gil Reece was capped 29 times by the Welsh men's national team.

    a. True

    b. False

13. How many appearances did Tony Kenworthy make in all competitions with the Blades?

a. 456

b. 382

c. 357

d. 328

14. Which national team capped David Carney 13 times while he was playing for Sheffield United?

    a. South Africa

    b. Australia

    c. Northern Ireland

    d. England

15. How many goals did John Lundstram score in the 2019-20 domestic league?

    a. 12

    b. 10

    c. 7

    d. 5

16. Jack Pickering played his entire professional career with the Blades.

    a. True

    b. False

17. Who appeared in 57 games in all competitions in 2014-15?

    a. Jose Baxter

    b. Ryan Flynn

    c. Louis Reed

    d. Michael Doyle

18. Who scored five goals in the 2001-02 domestic league?

    a. Michael Brown
    b. Bobby Ford
    c. Michael Tonge
    d. Jean-Philippe Javary

19. How many career games did Nick Montgomery play for the Blades?

    a. 350
    b. 376
    c. 399
    d. 434

20. Lee Evans recorded five assists in the 2017-18 Championship League.

    a. True
    b. False

QUIZ ANSWERS

1. B – Nick Montgomery

2. B – False

3. D – Stephen Quinn

4. C – Adrian Littlejohn

5. C – 13

6. A – Mansfield Town FC

7. A – True

8. B – 105

9. C – Northern Ireland

10. B – Mark Duffy

11. C – 12

12. A – True

13. C – 357

14. B – Australia

15. D – 5

16. A – True

17. D – Michael Doyle

18. A – Michael Brown

19. C – 399

20. B – False

DID YOU KNOW?

1. Ernest "Nudger" Needham joined Sheffield United in the Northern League in April 1891 and remained with the club for nearly two decades. The team joined the newly formed Football League Second Division in 1892-93, and Needham helped them finish their inaugural season as runners-up. Nicknamed "the Prince of half-backs," he was one of the team's first star players at both ends of the pitch. The English international was appointed club captain in 1895 and led the team to second place in the First Division in 1896-97 and went to the top of the league the next season. The Blades then won the FA Cup for the first time in 1898-99, finished as league runners-up in 1899-1900, reached the 1900-01 FA Cup final, and won the FA Cup in 1901-02. Needham retired in 1910 after scoring more than 60 goals in approximately 550 games. He was also a first-class cricket player, and his nephew, George Wright Needham, played pro soccer for several English clubs.

2. After beginning his career with amateur club Tunstall Cresswells, Albert Sturgess joined hometown Stoke City in 1902 and became a regular starter in 1905-06. Nicknamed "Hairpin," due to his wiry build, he joined Sheffield United with teammate George Gallimore in the summer of 1908. He formed an effective midfield partnership with George

Utley and Bill Brelsford and could play anywhere on the pitch, including emergency goalkeeper. Sturgess helped the side reach the 1913-14 FA Cup semifinals and then win the trophy the following season. He was appointed club captain in 1919 following the First World War and played nearly 400 games with the club record before joining Norwich City as club captain in July 1923 at the age of 40. He was also capped twice by England.

3. English international George Green was an England schoolboy international who began his career with hometown clubs Leamington St John's, Leamington Imperial, and Leamington Town in 1918-19 before joining Birmingham League side Nuneaton Town in 1921 as a professional. He joined First Division Sheffield United in May 1923 and helped the side win the 1925 FA Cup. He spent 11 seasons at Bramall Lane and wore the captain's armband for a spell until 1933. He played over 400 contests with the team and scored 11 goals before leaving for Leamington Town in July 1934.

4. Tony Currie was the first Sheffield United midfielder to win the club's Player of the Year award, in 1970-71, when the team finished as the Second Division runner-up. The former England Youth player was transferred to the Blades from Watford in February 1968 and scored in his debut at the age of 18. Nicknamed "Top Cat" by the club's fans, he was appointed captain in 1974. Currie scored over 65 goals in more than 350 games before joining Leeds United in June 1976 after Sheffield United was relegated.

The England international was voted the Blades' best player of all time at the club's 125th anniversary event in 2014, and there's a stand named in his honor at Bramall Lane. He was later named a club director. His nephew, Darren Currie, who played over 600 games in the Football League, was a co-manager of Sheffield United's under-23 team in 2021.

5. The second midfielder to be voted the Blades' Player of the Year in 1971-72 was English-born Welsh international Trevor Hockey. He turned professional with Bradford City in 1960 and debuted with the club at the age of 17. He was named Player of the Year for Birmingham City for 1968-69 and played over 200 times with the team, many of them as captain, before being transferred to Sheffield United for a reported £40,000 in January 1971. He quickly became a cult figure at Bramall Lane with his beard and Beatle-style haircut. Hockey helped the team earn promotion in 1970-71 as the Second Division runner-up. Hockey suffered a broken leg in February 1972 and left the team for Norwich City a year later. He later played and managed in Ireland and America and passed away of a heart attack shortly after playing in a five-a-side tournament in April 1987 at the age of 43.

6. Welsh international Dave Powell was the first non-English winner of the Blades' Player of the Year award, for the 1968-69 campaign. He played with Gwydir Rovers as a youth and joined Wrexham in January 1962. He played over 100 games with the Welsh team before

joining Sheffield United in September 1968 for a reported £28,500 fee. He was a regular starter for the next three seasons and a key player on the squad that earned promotion to the top-tier by finishing as the Second Division runner-up in 1970-71. However, he was sidelined for almost a year after suffering a knee injury and was released in September 1972. He then returned to Wales to play with Cardiff City. After hanging up his boots, Powell joined the South Wales Police and coached their soccer team.

7. Curtis Woodhouse began his career as a youth player with York City in 1994 before being transferred to Sheffield United in 1997. He made his first-team debut at the age of 17, became the club's youngest-ever captain when he was 19, and was voted the team's Player of the Year for 1998-99. He played four times for the England Under-21 Team and appeared in 122 matches for the Blades, scoring six goals, before being sold to Birmingham City for £1 million in February 2001. Woodhouse later embarked on a pro boxing career, compiled a record of 24-7 with 13 KOs, and became the British super-lightweight champion. He also became a soccer manager.

8. Nick Montgomery of Scotland was offered a two-year scholarship at Sheffield United as a youth and debuted as a first-team player in October 2000. He was an integral member of the 2005-06 squad that finished as the Championship League runner-up to reach the Premier League, although they were relegated after one season.

He was runner-up to Phil Jagielka in the club's Player of Year voting in 2005-06 and won the honor in 2009-10. The Blades were relegated to the third tier for the first time in over two decades in 2010-11, and Montgomery was loaned to Millwall in March 2012 for a month. He then helped the Blades reach the playoffs and left the club in August 2012, after playing just under 400 games, to play in Australia.

9. Republic of Ireland international Stephen Quinn kicked off his career with St Patrick's Athletic in the League of Ireland before moving to Bramall Lane in 2005. He spent part of the 2005-06 season on loan with Milton Keynes Dons and Rotherham United while his teammates were finishing as runners-up in the Championship League to earn promotion to the Premier League. He was named the team's Player of the Year for 2010-11, but the side was relegated, this time to the third tier. Quinn scored 22 goals in 237 outings with the Blades but was sold to Hull City in August 2012.

10. Scottish international John Fleck began his career with Glasgow Rangers and made his senior debut in 2008 at the age of 16. He arrived at Sheffield United in July 2016 from Coventry City and helped the club achieve promotion to the Premier League in 2016-17 by winning the third-tier title. He also shared the team's Player of the Year award with Billy Sharp that season. Fleck then won the trophy again for his fine play in 2017-18, and the following season, he helped the team return to the Premier League after a 12-

year absence by finishing as the runner-up in the Championship League. At the end of the 2020-21 season, he had scored 13 goals in 206 games for the Blades and was named to the PFA League One Team of the Year for 2016-17. Fleck is the nephew of former pro soccer player Robert Fleck.

CHAPTER 8:

SENSATIONAL STRIKERS & FORWARDS

QUIZ TIME!

1. Who appeared in the most career matches with the club?

   a. Fred Tunstall

   b. Jimmy Hagan

   c. Alan Woodward

   d. Billy Gillespie

2. Peter Ndlovu scored 37 goals in 88 caps for the Zimbabwe men's national team.

   a. True

   b. False

3. Who played in 41 games in the 1992-93 Premier League campaign?

   a. Alan Cork

   b. Franz Carr

   c. Mike Lake

   d. Brian Deane

4. How many goals did Carl Asaba score in the 2002-03 domestic league?

    a. 15

    b. 11

    c. 7

    d. 5

5. Who tallied eight assists in the 2014-15 League One season?

    a. Jamal Campbell-Ryce

    b. Steve Davies

    c. Marc McNulty

    d. Jamie Murphy

6. Tony Currie joined Sheffield United from which outfit?

    a. Stoke City FC

    b. Norwich City FC

    c. Watford FC

    d. Leeds United

7. Oliver McBurnie played in all 38 games in the 2019-20 Premier League.

    a. True

    b. False

8. How many appearances did Brian Deane make for the side in all competitions?

    a. 241

    b. 275

c. 316

d. 354

9. Jostein Flo was capped 26 times by what men's national team while playing for Sheffield United?

   a. Norway

   b. Iceland

   c. Denmark

   d. Switzerland

10. Who scored 14 goals in all competitions in 2012-13?

    a. Davie Kitson

    b. Chris Porter

    c. Nick Blackman

    d. Shaun Miller

11. Who scored five goals in the 2006-07 domestic league?

    a. Danny Weber

    b. John Stead

    c. Christian Nadé

    d. Colin Kazim-Richards

12. Alan Woodward played his entire professional career with Sheffield United.

    a. True

    b. False

13. How many appearances did Tony Agana make in all competitions with the Blades?

    a. 42

    b. 133

c. 154

d. 378

14. Which of these players did NOT score five goals in the 2010-11 Championship League?

    a. Darius Henderson

    b. Richard Cresswell

    c. Mark Yeates

    d. Daniel Bogdanović

15. How many goals did Billy Sharp contribute in the 2017-18 domestic league?

    a. 6

    b. 10

    c. 13

    d. 17

16. Petr Katchouro was capped 10 times by the Belarusian men's national team while playing for Sheffield United.

    a. True

    b. False

17. Peter Ndlovu left the Blades to join what team?

    a. Santos FC

    b. Leicester City FC

    c. Mamelodi Sundowns FC

    d. Birmingham City FC

18. How many appearances did Alan Woodward make in all competitions with Sheffield United?

a. 505

b. 530

c. 583

d. 640

19. Which national team was Luton Shelton capped by nine times while playing for the Blades?

a. Jamaica

b. England

c. Trinidad and Tobago

d. Bahamas

20. Darius Henderson was shown two red cards in the 2008-09 domestic league.

a. True

b. False

QUIZ ANSWERS

1. C – Alan Woodward

2. A – True

3. D – Brian Deane

4. B – 11

5. D – Jamie Murphy

6. C – Watford FC

7. B – False

8. B – 275

9. A – Norway

10. C – Nick Blackman

11. B – John Stead

12. B – False

13. C – 154

14. A – Darius Henderson

15. C – 13

16. A – True

17. C – Mamelodi Sundowns FC

18. D – 640

19. A – Jamaica

20. A – True

DID YOU KNOW?

1. Center-forward Harry Hammond played with Edge Hill and Everton before joining Sheffield United in the Northern League in the summer of 1891. He led the side in scoring with 22 goals in 1892-93 when the club joined the Football League's newly formed Second Division, earned promotion as runner-up, and won their playoff contest. He notched the team's first hat-trick in its very first Football League match and scored five goals, and four goals in a game later in the campaign. Hammond also led the squad in scoring in 1894-95 and 1895-96 and became the first Blades player to receive a red card during a league game. He scored over 60 goals for the club in fewer than 175 games before joining New Brighton Tower in the Lancashire League in 1897 after helping Sheffield United finish as the First Division runner-up in 1896-97.

2. Credited with scoring 114 goals in just under 200 matches for the Blades was England international Arthur Brown. He joined the club in the summer of 1902 from Gainsborough Trinity and led the side in scoring for five straight seasons, from 1903-04 to 1907-08, with a career-high 22 goals in both 1904-05 and 1906-07. He also led the First Division in 1904-05. His goal-scoring expertise led to interest from other clubs, and Brown was sold to Sunderland in June 1908 for a reported £1,000.

3. Colin Collindridge was working as a miner and playing amateur soccer when Wolverhampton Wanderers offered him a trial in 1937. However, he signed with Rotherham United a year later before joining Barugh Green in 1938. Sheffield United spotted him and signed him as a professional in January 1939. He played with the Blades and several other sides during World War II when he was in the Royal Air Force and established himself as a regular starter when the Football League resumed in 1946 following the war. Collindridge played as an outside-left and center-forward and scored 59 goals in just over 150 games before signing with Nottingham Forest in August 1950.

4. Alf Ringstead of County Dublin, Ireland, was the son of English jockey Charlie Ringstead. He joined Sheffield United in November 1950 along with fellow winger Derek Hawksworth. He had served in the British Army in India and was working as an upholsterer when he decided to give pro soccer a shot. He was a prolific scorer, with 109 goals in 271 games during his Blades career, and led the side in scoring in 1951-52 and again in 1952-53 when the team won the Second Division. The Republic of Ireland international scored seven goals in 20 outings for his country and joined Mansfield Town in 1959.

5. Welsh international Gil Reece represented his homeland 29 times, scoring two goals, and scored 67 times in just under 250 outings with Sheffield United. He joined the club from Newport County in April 1965 but missed

much of the 1966-67 season with a broken leg. After helping the team finish as the Second Division runner-up in 1970-71, the former plumber left for his homeland when he joined Cardiff City in September 1972 along with Blades teammate Dave Powell. Alan Warboys came to Bramall Lane in the transaction. Reece had his right leg amputated in 2000 due to an illness and passed away at the age of 61, three years later. He was the brother of Welsh boxer Leonard "Luggie" Reece and grandfather of Welsh Rugby League international Lewis Reece.

6. With 119 goals in 275 games, Brian Deane ranks as one of the Blades' all-time leading scorers. He arrived in 1988 from Doncaster Rovers and helped the side finish as the Third Division runner-up in 1988-89 and the Second Division runner-up the following season. He led the team in scoring for four straight seasons starting in 1989-90, was voted the team's Player of the Year for 1990-91, and scored the first Premier League goal ever for the club. He joined Leeds United in 1993 for a reported £2.9 million fee to set a Leeds and Sheffield United transfer record at the time. Deane returned to Sheffield United in July 1997 and led the club in scoring while helping it reach the second-tier playoffs. He joined Benfica at the end of the season, played for a few other clubs in England, and also played in Australia before once again joining the Blades in December 2005. Deane played just two league games and retired. He later managed in Norway and is now a part-owner of Ferizaj in the Kosovo Superleague.

7. Pyotr Pyatrovich Kachura was a Belarus international who was commonly known as Petr or Peter Katchouro during his playing career. He kicked his career off with hometown team Dinamo Minsk and left in July 1996 for Sheffield United for a reported £650,000 transfer fee. He tallied 14 goals in his first season to help the side reach the second-tier playoffs, where they lost the final to Crystal Palace on a last-minute goal. However, he was voted the team's Player of the Year for 1996-97. Injuries limited him to just 16 games in 1997-98, and the team reached the playoffs again. He suffered a punctured lung the next campaign but managed to score six goals in 16 outings. Kachura left in March 2000 for Chinese club Chengdu Wuniu on a free transfer after scoring 23 goals in 121 games. He later managed several teams in his homeland.

8. Billy Sharp debuted with hometown Sheffield United in 2004-05 and was then loaned to Rushden and Diamonds in January 2005. He joined Scunthorpe United later in 2005 and scored 56 goals in 95 games before the Blades decided they wanted him back. He returned in July 2007 but scored just 13 times in 64 matches before joining Doncaster Rovers in 2009. Sharp returned to Bramall Lane again in July 2015 and led the side in scoring in 2015-16, 2016-17, and 2018-19, reaching 30 goals in 2016-17. After being appointed club captain, he led the team to the third-tier title in 2016-17 and to the runner-up spot in the second tier in 2018-19. With the Blades, Sharp was named to the PFA League One Team of the Year in 2016-17 and

the Championship League Team of the Year in 2018-19 and was the League One Player of the Year for 2016-17. He was also voted Sheffield United's Player of the Year for 2015-16 and shared the award in 2016-17. Sharp had scored 111 goals with the team by the end of the 2020-21 season.

9. The 1988-89 Sheffield United Player of the Year was striker Tony Agana, who arrived at Bramall Lane in January 1988 from Watford. He scored in his debut and played 13 games over the remainder of the season, but the team was relegated. Agana formed an effective striking partnership with newcomer Brian Deane and notched 24 league goals in 46 appearances and 31 goals in all competitions. He helped the side finish as the Third Division runner-up that season and Second Division runner-up the next campaign when he tallied a dozen goals, including a pair in the promotion-clinching game. Agana netted 52 goals in 154 matches before joining Notts County in November 1991 for a reported £685,000, which was a Blades-record transfer fee at the time. He later returned to Sheffield United to work with the club's match day hospitality team.

10. After playing with several English clubs since 2004, Dave McGoldrick ended up with Sheffield United in July 2018 from Ipswich Town after impressing manager Chris Wilder during a week-long trial period. He scored 15 goals in his first season and was voted the side's Player of the Year as the Blades earned promotion to the Premier

League as second-tier runners-up. However, he scored just four goals in 2019-20. McGoldrick bounced back with nine goals in 2020-21 to lead the club in scoring, but they were relegated at the end of the season. By the end of the campaign, he had scored 28 goals in 115 outings with the club. In 2014, McGoldrick, who is adopted, discovered he was eligible to play for the Republic of Ireland after researching his family tree and has scored one goal in 14 matches with the team.

CHAPTER 9:

NOTABLE TRANSFERS & SIGNINGS

QUIZ TIME!

1. Who has been the Blades' most expensive transfer signing as of June 2021?

    a. Rhian Brewster

    b. Aaron Ramsdale

    c. Oliver McBurnie

    d. Sander Berge

2. Sheffield United acquired 15 different players on free transfers in 2012-13.

    a. True

    b. False

3. Who was the Blades' most expensive transfer signing in 2018-19?

    a. Richard Stearman

    b. Lee Evans

    c. John Egan

    d. Oliver Norwood

4. The Blades sold what player to Stoke City FC for a transfer fee of £3.6 million in 2008-09?

   a. Chris Armstrong
   b. Jon Stead
   c. Rob Hulse
   d. James Beattie

5. Who was sold for Sheffield United's highest received transfer fee as of June 2021?

   a. Phil Jagielka
   b. David Brooks
   c. Kyle Naughton
   d. Claude Davis

6. Sheffield United signed Sander Berge from which club?

   a. KRC Genk
   b. Asker SK
   c. KSC Lokeren
   d. Odds BK

7. The club acquired defender Rob Kozluk from Peterborough United in 1999 for £2 million.

   a. True
   b. False

8. How much did the Blades pay to acquire Aaron Ramsdale?

   a. £22 million
   b. £18.45 million

c. £15 million

d. £13.8 million

9. Who was the club's most expensive transfer signing in 2014-15?

   a. Joe Baxter

   b. Billy Sharp

   c. John Brayford

   d. Marc McNulty

10. Which club did the Blades transfer David Brooks to?

    a. Lille OSC

    b. Atletico Madrid

    c. Manchester City FC

    d. Bournemouth AFC

11. What was the transfer fee Sheffield United received for selling Phil Jagielka?

    a. £11 million

    b. £7.76 million

    c. £5.4 million

    d. £4 million

12. Sheffield United signed Oliver Burke from La Liga club Deportivo Alavés.

    a. True

    b. False

13. How much did the Blades pay to acquire Sander Berge?

    a. £20.7 million

    b. £18 million

c. £16.6 million

d. £14 million

14. Which player did Sheffield United sell to Birmingham City FC for a fee of £1.98 million in 2016-17?

a. Ché Adams

b. Dominic Calvert-Lewin

c. Graham Kelly

d. Matt Done

15. Sheffield United sold David Brooks for what transfer fee?

a. £16 million

b. £15.25 million

c. £13 million

d. £10.17 million

16. The Blades acquired defender John Flynn from Workington in 1969.

a. True

b. False

17. Which club did the Blades sell Phil Jagielka to?

a. Liverpool FC

b. Everton FC

c. Aston Villa

d. Newcastle United

18. What was the transfer fee Sheffield United paid to sign Rhian Brewster?

a. £16.5 million

b. £19 million

c. £23.4 million

d. £35 million

19. Who was the Blades' most expensive transfer acquisition in 2005-06?

a. Colin Kazim-Richards

b. Paul Ifill

c. Geoff Horsfield

d. Ade Akinbiyi

20. Sheffield United sold both Kyle Walker and Kyle Naughton to Tottenham Hotspur for £5.31 million each in 2009-10.

a. True

b. False

QUIZ ANSWERS

1. A – Rhian Brewster

2. B – False

3. C – John Egan

4. D – James Beattie

5. B – David Brooks

6. A – KRC Genk

7. B – False

8. B – £18.45 million

9. C – John Brayford

10. D – Bournemouth AFC

11. C – £5.4 million

12. B – False

13. A – £20.7 million

14. A – Ché Adams

15. D – £10.17 million

16. A – True

17. B – Everton FC

18. C – £23.4 million

19. D – Ade Akinbiyi

20. A – True

DID YOU KNOW?

1. The five highest transfer fees paid by Sheffield United as of June 9, 2021, are: forward Rhian Brewster from Liverpool for £23.4 million in 2020-21; midfielder Sander Berge from KRC Genk for £20.7 million in 2019-20; goalkeeper Aaron Ramsdale from AFC Bournemouth for £18.45 million in 2020-21; forward Oliver McBurnie from Swansea City for £17.19 million in 2019-20; forward Lys Mousset from AFC Bournemouth for £9.99 million in 2019-20.

2. The five highest transfer fees received by the club as of June 9, 2021, are: winger David Brooks to AFC Bournemouth for £10.17 million in 2018-19; defender Phil Jagielka to Everton FC for £5.4 million in 2007-08; defender Kyle Naughton to Tottenham Hotspur for £5.31 million in 2009-10; defender Kyle Walker to Tottenham Hotspur for £5.31 million in 2009-10; defender Claude Davis to Derby County for £4.05 million in 2007-08.

3. The Blades' most expensive transfer acquisition so far was forward Rhian Brewster from Liverpool for £23.4 million in October 2020. He signed a five-year contract, but the deal reportedly includes a buy-back clause of £40 million which is valid June 30, 2023. He played 30 games in all competitions in 2020-21, and the club was relegated from the Premier League. Brewster is an England youth

international and has represented the nation at various youth levels but remains eligible to play senior national games for Turkey because his mother is a Turkish Cypriot. He's also eligible to represent Barbados, where his father hails from. He made a name for himself at the 2017 FIFA Under-17 World Cup by winning the event's Golden Boot with eight goals, as England won the cup. He was also awarded the Bronze Ball for his individual performances.

4. Norwegian international midfielder Sander Berge played youth soccer in his homeland before joining Genk in Belgium in January 2017. He arrived at Bramall Lane on January 30, 2020, and signed a 4.5-year contract. His £20.7 million fee was a Blades record at the time. He played 16 games for the club in 2019-20 and 2020-21, scoring once each season. However, the side was relegated following his second campaign. Berge comes from a basketball-playing family: His father, Swedish mother, and older brother have all played the sport at the international level. In addition, his grandfather Ragnar Berge was a pro soccer player who was capped once by Norway.

5. Goalkeeper Aaron Ramsdale started his career with Sheffield United in 2013 as a youth and posted a clean sheet in his debut in a 2016 FA Cup match. He joined AFC Bournemouth in January 2017 for a fee of £846,000 and spent time on loan with Chesterfield and AFC Wimbledon. He won the Wimbledon Young Player of the Season award for 2018-19 before returning to Bournemouth, where he

won the 2019-20 Player of the Year award as voted by the club's supporters. In August 2020, Ramsdale joined Sheffield United for an £18.45 million fee and was named the side's Player of the Year and Young Player of the Year for 2020-21, even though they were relegated from the Premier League. Ramsdale has represented England at under-18, under-19, under-20, and under-21 levels.

6. Scottish international forward Oliver McBurnie cost the Blades a fee of £17.19 million when they acquired him from Swansea City in July 2019. This was a Sheffield United record fee at the time as well as a record for a transfer involving a Scottish player. He finished the 2019-20 campaign as the team's joint highest scorer with Lys Mousset at six goals each but scored just one goal in 25 outings in 2020-21 when the club was relegated. McBurnie was fined £28,500 and banned from driving for 16 months in July 2020 and, in February 2021, offered to pay for the funeral of a 26-year-old Swansea City fan who had passed away.

7. Winger David Brooks was born in England and represented the nation at the under-20 level before deciding to play senior international soccer with Wales. He spent a decade as a youngster with Manchester City before arriving at the Blades' youth academy in 2014. He debuted with the first-team in August 2016 and was chosen to play for the senior Welsh side four days later. Brooks didn't play regularly with the side until 2017-18 when he scored three goals in 33 games. He was then

transferred to AFC Bournemouth in July 2018 for a fee of £10.17 million to set a new Sheffield United record.

8. Defender Phil Jagielka joined Sheffield United in 1998 at 15 years of age, made his senior debut two years later, and established himself as a regular in 2002-03. By the end of 2006-07, Jagielka had played in 133 straight league games, including every match in the 2004-05 and 2005-06 seasons and every minute of the 2006-07 campaign. The team was relegated from the Premier League at the end of 2006-07, and he was sold to Everton in 2007 for a Sheffield United record of £5.4 million at the time. Jagielka rejoined the Blades in July 2019 on a free transfer and played with the team in 2020-21 as a 38-year-old. With Sheffield United, he has been named the Football League Championship Player of the Year for 2005-06; the PFA First Division Team of the Year for 2003-04; the PFA Championship League Team of the Year for 2005-06; the club's Player of the Year for 2004-05, 2005-06, and 2006-07; and has appeared in more than 300 games with just over 20 goals scored.

9. Defender Kyle Walker kicked off his pro career with his hometown club, Sheffield United, after joining at the age of seven. He was loaned to Northampton Town for three months in November 2008 and made his Blades debut in January 2009. He became the youngest Sheffield United player to appear at Wembley Stadium when the team reached the playoff final that season. After just seven appearances in all competitions, Walker was sold to

Tottenham Hotspur in July 2009 for £5.31 million and loaned back to the Blades for the 2009-10 season. Walker went on to become a regular England international and has won several individual and team awards with Manchester City after being sold to the club by Tottenham for £47.43 million in 2017. He was still with Man City as of June 2021.

10. Oddly enough, another Sheffield-born right-back named Kyle also started his career with the Blades and was sold to Tottenham Hotspur in July 2009 for the exact same fee as Kyle Walker, £5.31 million. In fact, Kyle Naughton and Kyle Walker were transferred to the Spurs together. Naughton also joined the club as a 7-year-old. He was loaned to Scottish Premier League team Gretna in January 2008 and made his senior debut for Sheffield United the following season. He played all 50 games in 2008-09, was voted the team's Young Player of the Year, was runner-up to Matthew Kilgallon as Player of the Year, and was included in the Championship PFA Team of the Year. He then joined the Spurs and was sold to Swansea City in January 2015 for £5.94 million. He was still there in June 2021.

CHAPTER 10:

DOMESTIC COMPETITION

QUIZ TIME!

1. How many divisional titles has Sheffield United won in the Football League as of 2021?

   a. 1
   b. 4
   c. 8
   d. 6

2. The Blades have never won a League Cup as of 2021.

   a. True
   b. False

3. Which season did Sheffield United win its first FA Cup?

   a. 1924-25
   b. 1904-05
   c. 1898-99
   d. 1893-94

4. What was the first trophy Sheffield United won?

a. Northern League championship

b. Sheffield Challenge Cup

c. Football League Second Division championship

d. Wharncliffe Charity Cup

5. How many times have the Blades been second-tier Division Two/Championship League runners-up as of 2021?

a. 4

b. 10

c. 2

d. 7

6. Which club did Sheffield United face in its first FA Cup final?

a. Stoke City FC

b. Derby County FC

c. Liverpool FC

d. Preston North End

7. Sheffield United shared the honors of the 1898 Sheriff London Charity Shield with Corinthian FC.

a. True

b. False

8. Which round did Sheffield United reach in the 2014-15 League Cup?

a. Second round

b. Third round

c. Quarterfinal

d. Semifinal

9. How many FA Cups have the Blades won as of 2021?

   a. 4

   b. 7

   c. 2

   d. 5

10. Sheffield United played what club in their first FA Cup match?

   a. Burnley FC

   b. Wolverhampton Wanderers

   c. Bootle FC

   d. Lincoln City FC

11. How many points did Sheffield United tally to win the 1945-46 Football League North?

   a. 71

   b. 67

   c. 60

   d. 52

12. In their first year competing for the League Cup in 1960-61, the Blades reached the semifinals.

   a. True

   b. False

13. How many times did the team outright win the Sheffield & Hallamshire County Cup?

   a. 25

   b. 21

c. 17

d. 12

14. Which season did Sheffield United win its first championship in the top-flight of the Football League?

    a. 1921-22

    b. 1902-03

    c. 1899-1900

    d. 1897-98

15. The side reached what round of the 1990-91 Full Members' Cup in the North Section?

    a. First round

    b. Third round

    c. Quarterfinal

    d. Final

16. Sheffield United was the fourth team to win a championship in all top four divisions of the Football League.

    a. True

    b. False

17. Which squad did Sheffield United play in the 1924-25 FA Cup final?

    a. Leicester City FC

    b. Southampton FC

    c. Blackburn Rovers FC

    d. Cardiff City FC

18. Who captained the Blades to their first FA Cup final?

    a. Jimmy Simmons
    b. Fred Priest
    c. George Utley
    d. Ernest Needham

19. How many times has the outfit finished as runner-up in the top-tier First Division/Premier League as of 2020-21?

    a. 5
    b. 2
    c. 4
    d. 1

20. The Blades have played in three FA Charity Shield matches as of 2021.

    a. True
    b. False

QUIZ ANSWERS

1. B – 4

2. A – True

3. C – 1898-99

4. B – Sheffield Challenge Cup

5. D – 7

6. B – Derby County FC

7. A – True

8. D – Semifinal

9. A – 4

10. A – Burnley FC

11. C – 60

12. B – False

13. B – 21

14. D – 1897-98

15. C – Quarterfinal

16. A – True

17. D – Cardiff City FC

18. D – Ernest Needham

19. B – 2

20. B – False

DID YOU KNOW?

1. The club has won championships in all top four divisions of the Football League, becoming the fourth team to do so, and has won four FA Cups. However, the side has yet to win a League Cup. In addition, Sheffield United was won the Football League North title in 1945-46 just after World War II ended and just before the Football League resumed play. The side also shared the Sheriff of London Charity Shield in 1898.

2. Sheffield United has never played in a UEFA-sanctioned competition as of 2021 but did compete in the non-sanctioned Texaco Cup/Anglo-Scottish cup event. The team played in this tournament for straight seasons, from 1972-73 to 1980-81, with their best finish coming in 1979-80 when they reached the semifinals. However, they were beaten 4-0 on aggregate by St. Mirren of Scotland after drawing 0-0 at home in the first leg and losing the second leg 4-0 away.

3. The Blades captured the top-tier First Division title in the Football League in 1897-98 and finished as runners-up in 1896-97 and 1899-1900. They hoisted the second-tier Second Division championship in 1952-53 and finished as runners-up in 1892-93, 1938-39, 1960-61, 1970-71, and 1989-90, as well as being runners-up in the second-tier Championship League in 2005-06 and 2018-19. The Blades

won the third-tier League One title in 2016-17 and were third-tier Third Division runners-up in 1988-89. The club also won the fourth-tier Fourth Division in 1981-82.

4. The FA Cup was won by Sheffield United in 1898-99, 1901-02, 1914-15, and 1924-25. The team finished as runner-up in 1900-01 and 1935-36. The furthest the team has advanced in the League Cup was to the semifinals in 2002-03 and 2014-15.

5. Sheffield United beat Derby County 4-1 at London's Crystal Palace in the 1898-99 FA Cup in front of 73,833 fans. They drew Southampton 1-1 at Crystal Palace in the 1901-02 event, with 74,479 supporters on hand, and then won the replay 2-1 at the same venue with 33,068 in attendance. The 1914-15 FA Cup was played at Old Trafford in Manchester, with 49,557 fans in the stands to witness Sheffield United down Chelsea 3-0. The Blades' last FA Cup triumph came in 1924-25 when they edged Cardiff 1-0 at Wembley Stadium in London with 91,763 fans as witnesses.

6. The side drew Tottenham Hotspur 2-2 in the 1900-01 FA Cup final at Crystal Palace in front of what was then a record crowd of 110,820. A replay was held a week later at Burnden Park in Bolton, with just 20,470 fans in attendance to see Spurs win 3-1. Sheffield United also lost the 1935-36 final when they were blanked 1-0 by Arsenal at Wembley in front of a crowd of 93,384.

7. The Sheriff of London Charity Shield was also known as the Dewar Shield and was played annually between the

best amateur and best professional clubs in England. The professional team was either the Football League champion or FA Cup winner from the previous season, while the amateurs were usually represented by Corinthian. Proceeds from the match were given to hospitals and charities, and the event later evolved into the FA Charity Shield and then the FA Community Shield. Sheffield United drew Corinthian 0-0 in the first Charity Shield ever, and the replay ended in a 1-1 draw as both clubs shared the honor.

8. The Blades' longest ventures into the League Cup came in 2002-03 and 2014-15. The squad beat Liverpool 2-1 at home in the first leg of the 2002-03 semifinals, with 30,095 fans in attendance. However, they were beaten 2-0 in extra time in the second leg in Liverpool in front of 43,837 fans to lose 3-2 on aggregate. In 2014-15, Sheffield United was beaten 1-0 away in the first leg to Tottenham Hotspur with 35,323 fans on hand and drew the second leg 2-2 at home with a crowd of 30,236 in the stadium to lose 3-2 on aggregate.

9. After the 2020-21 season, Sheffield United has competed in the Football League for 118 campaigns. The team has spent 62 of those seasons in the top-tier, 44 campaigns in the second tier, 11 seasons in the third tier, and just one campaign in the fourth tier of the league's pyramid.

10. Sheffield United has appeared in the divisional playoffs on eight occasions as of 2021. They competed in the second-tier tournaments in 1987-88, 1996-97, 1997-98,

2002-03, and 2008-09, and in the third-tier showdowns in 2011-12, 2012-13, and 2014-15. The team finished as runner-up in 1996-97, 2002-03, 2008-09, and 2011-12 but has never won a playoff tournament.

CHAPTER 11:

CLUB RECORDS

QUIZ TIME!

1. What is the most wins Sheffield United has recorded in a domestic league season as of 2020-21?

    a. 22

    b. 34

    c. 28

    d. 30

2. The Blades' most consecutive wins in a domestic league season was 11 in 1903-04.

    a. True

    b. False

3. Who has received the most international caps while playing for Sheffield United?

    a. Peter Ndlovu

    b. Jostein Flo

    c. Billy Gillespie

    d. Alan Kelly

4. The Blades' biggest away victory in a league match was 10-0 against what club?

    a. Newcastle United
    b. Middlesbrough FC
    c. Port Vale FC
    d. Crewe Alexandra FC

5. What is the most goals Sheffield United scored in a domestic league season as of 2020-21?

    a. 90
    b. 97
    c. 102
    d. 111

6. Who took a club-record 54 penalty kicks during his Blades career?

    a. Jock Dodds
    b. Colin Morris
    c. Bill Dearden
    d. Ched Evans

7. Keith Gillespie shares the record for the fastest red card shown to a substitute, receiving it in zero seconds because the game had not yet officially restarted.

    a. True
    b. False

8. What is the most consecutive home games Sheffield United has won in a domestic league season as of 2020-21?

a. 17

b. 14

c. 11

d. 8

9. Who scored seven goals from the penalty spot in seven attempts in his Sheffield United career?

a. Peter Duffield

b. Steve Charles

c. John Tudor

d. Andy Walker

10. The Blades' biggest league defeat was 10-3 to what club?

a. Chelsea FC

b. Middlesbrough FC

c. West Bromwich Albion

d. Sheffield Wednesday

11. What is the most points Sheffield United ever recorded in a domestic league season as of 2020-21?

a. 83

b. 96

c. 89

d. 100

12. The highest recorded official attendance at Bramall Lane was 50,587.

a. True

b. False

13. Who once made 203 consecutive appearances in domestic league matches?

    a. George Green
    b. Gerry Summers
    c. Jack Smith
    d. Tony Kenworthy

14. What is the longest stretch of games the Blades have gone without losing in the domestic league?

    a. 13
    b. 26
    c. 17
    d. 22

15. Sheffield United set its home attendance record in a match against what club?

    a. Manchester United
    b. Swansea City FC
    c. Leeds United
    d. Tottenham Hotspur

16. Tony Currie received the most caps by the English men's national team while playing for Sheffield United.

    a. True
    b. False

17. What is the most losses the Blades have suffered in a domestic league season as of 2020-21?

    a. 33
    b. 29

c. 25

d. 21

18. Who was the youngest player to score for Sheffield United as of June 2021, at 17 years and 61 days?

    a. Jonathan Forte

    b. Alan Woodward

    c. Daniel Jebbison

    d. Regan Slater

19. Sheffield United's biggest defeat in a League Cup match was 13-0 to what club?

    a. Liverpool FC

    b. Manchester City FC

    c. Fulham FC

    d. Bolton Wanderers FC

20. The Blades had a club-record 19 different players score at least one goal in the 2008-09 domestic league.

    a. True

    b. False

QUIZ ANSWERS

1. D – 30

2. B – False

3. A – Peter Ndlovu

4. C – Port Vale FC

5. C – 102

6. B – Colin Morris

7. A – True

8. C – 11

9. A – Peter Duffield

10. B – Middlesbrough FC

11. D – 100

12. B – False

13. C – Jack Smith

14. D – 22

15. C – Leeds United

16. B – False

17. B – 29

18. D – Regan Slater

19. D – Bolton Wanderers FC

20. A – True

DID YOU KNOW?

1. The record attendance for the Bramall Lane ground is 68,287, which was set at an FA Cup fifth-round match between Sheffield United and Leeds United on February 15, 1936. The ground was extensively renovated in later years following the Taylor Report and is now an all-seater venue with a capacity of 32,050. Defender Joe Shaw holds the club record for official appearances in all non-wartime competitions at 713, with 632 of these coming in league action between 1945 and 1966. The high mark for goals in a league season was set by Jimmy Dunne, who scored 41 goals in 41 games in the First Division in 1930-31.

2. The top 12 Blades players in games played for the team are: Joe Shaw, 714 (1945-66); Alan Hodgkinson, 674 (1954-71); Alan Woodward, 640 (1964-78); Ernest Needham, 544 (1891-1910); Len Badger, 541 (1962-76); Billy Gillespie, 507 (1911-31); Graham Shaw, 497 (1952-67); Fred Tunstall, 491 (1920-32); Cec Coldwell, 477 (1952-66); George Green, 438 (1923-34); Eddie Colquhoun, 433 (1968-78); and Jimmy Hagan, 407 (1938-57).

3. The team's record league win was 10-0 away over Port Vale in the Second Division in December 1892 and 10-0 at home over Burnley FC in the First Division in January 1929. Their biggest league defeat was 10-3 away to Middlesbrough in the First Division in November 1933.

The record cup win was 6-0 at home over Leyton Orient in the first round of the FA Cup in November 2016, while their record cup defeat was 13-0 at home versus Bolton Wanderers in the second round of the FA Cup in February 1890.

4. The most points accumulated in a league campaign with two points for a win was 60 in the Second Division in 1952-53. The most points taken with three points for a win was 100 in third-tier League One in 2016-17. The most goals scored in a league campaign was 102 in the First Division One in 1925-26, while the most wins posted was 30 in 46 games in League One in 2016-17.

5. The highest percentage of wins in a league season is 72.7% in the Second Division in 1892-93, with 16 victories in 22 games. The fewest points posted by the Blades in a Football League season was 22 in 42 games in the First Division in 1975-76. The longest winless streak in team history was 20 games in the Premier League between 2019-20 and 2020-21.

6. The most consecutive league wins by Sheffield United was eight, in 1892-93, 1903-04, 1945-46, 1957-58, 1960-61, 2005-06, 2016-17, and 2017-18. The most home wins in a row was 11 in the Second Division in 1960-61, while the most successive away wins was six in the Second Division in 1892-93. The club's longest unbeaten streak in the league was 22 matches in the First Division in 1899-1900. The longest home unbeaten streak was 26 in the Fourth

and Third Divisions between 1981-82 and 1982-83. The longest away undefeated string was 17 contests in the Championship League and Premier League between 2018-19 and 2019-20.

7. The most consecutive appearances by a player was 203 by Jack Smith between 1935 and 1948. The most hat-tricks in a Blades career was 20 by Harry Johnson Jr., with 18 of them coming in the Football League and the other two in the FA Cup. The most league goals in a game was five by Harry Hammond versus Bootle in the Second Division in 1892 and Harry Johnson Jr. versus West Ham United in the First Division in December 1927. The club record for scoring in consecutive games is 12 set by Jimmy Dunne in the First Division in 1931-32.

8. The oldest player to appear in a match for Sheffield United was Jimmy Hagan, at the age of 39 years and 236 days, while the youngest was Louis Reed, at 16 years and 257 days. The youngest goal scorer was Regan Slater, at 17 years and 60 days, versus Grimsby Town in a Football League Trophy game on November 9, 2016. The youngest league goal scorer was Simon Stainrod, at 17 years and 61 days, versus Norwich City in the First Division on April 3, 1976.

9. The most-capped player for a British national while playing for Sheffield United was Billy Gillespie, with all 25 of his appearances for Ireland coming as a member of the Blades. The most-capped player overall while playing

for the Blades was Peter Ndlovu, with 26 of his 81 outings for Zimbabwe coming while at Sheffield United.

10. The highest average home league attendance for a season for Sheffield United was 35,094 in the First Division in 1947-48. Before the Covid-19 pandemic struck in 2020, the lowest official league attendance was 4,014, versus Nottingham Forest in the Second Division in April 1935. The lowest FA Cup crowd was 5,987, versus Crewe Alexandra in November 2014, and the smallest League Cup crowd was 3,531, versus Colchester United in September 2000. The lowest away league attendance was 1,325 at Wimbledon FC in the First Division in April 2003. The lowest away FA Cup crowd was 2,509 at Colchester United in November 2013, and the smallest away League Cup attendance was 1,379 at Lincoln City in September 2000.

CHAPTER 12:

TOP SCORERS

QUIZ TIME!

1. Which player has scored the most career goals for the club in all competitions?

    a. Keith Edwards

    b. Alan Woodward

    c. Harry Johnson Jr.

    d. Doc Pace

2. Sheffield United has had 11 different players win a Golden Boot in the top-flight of the Football League as of 2020-21.

    a. True

    b. False

3. Who led the Blades in scoring in three of their first four seasons in the Football League?

    a. Harry Hammond

    b. Sandy Wallace

    c. Fred Davies

    d. James Duncan

4. Who scored the most goals in a single domestic league season?

    a. Jimmy Dunne
    b. Alan Woodward
    c. Fred Tunstall
    d. Colin Morris

5. How many goals did Brian Deane score in all competitions with Sheffield United?

    a. 99
    b. 106
    c. 114
    d. 119

6. Who was the first Sheffield United player to lead the top-tier in scoring in the Football League?

    a. Bill Dearden
    b. Colin Collindridge
    c. Derek Pace
    d. Arthur Brown

7. Sheffield United has had 16 different players reach the 100-goal mark in all competitions as of June 2021.

    a. True
    b. False

8. How many goals did Brian Deane score to lead the Blades in the 1992-93 Premier League?

    a. 8
    b. 19

c. 10

d. 15

9. Who led the club with 12 goals in the 2008-09 domestic league campaign?

   a. Stephen Quinn

   b. James Beattie

   c. Darius Henderson

   d. David Cotterill

10. Who led the side in scoring in all competitions in five consecutive seasons, from 1981-82 to 1985-86?

   a. Keith Edwards

   b. Colin Morris

   c. Steve Charles

   d. Tony Kenworthy

11. Who captured the 2016-17 League One Golden Boot award with 30 goals?

   a. John Fleck

   b. Leon Clarke

   c. Billy Sharp

   d. Kieron Freeman

12. Harry Johnson Jr. was the first player to score a club-record five goals in a domestic league match.

   a. True

   b. False

13. How many goals did Alan Woodward score in all competitions with Sheffield United?

a. 178

b. 191

c. 202

d. 211

14. Which two players led the Blades with 10 goals each in the 2005-06 Championship League?

    a. Paul Ifill and Danny Webber

    b. Phil Jagielka and Steve Kabba

    c. Alan Quinn and Neil Shipperley

    d. Neil Shipperley and Danny Webber

15. How many goals did Ched Evans score in all competitions with the squad in 2011-12?

    a. 35

    b. 29

    c. 24

    d. 20

16. Derek Pace led the Blades in scoring in all competitions in seven consecutive seasons, 1957-58 to 1963-64.

    a. True

    b. False

17. What two players led the club with 11 goals each in the 2012-13 domestic league?

    a. Dave Kitson and Ryan Flynn

    b. Chris Porter and Shaun Miller

    c. Nick Blackman and Dave Kitson

    d. Shaun Miller and Neill Collins

18. How many goals did Harry Johnson Jr. score in all competitions with the Blades?

    a. 209
    b. 220
    c. 233
    d. 252

19. Who led Sheffield United with 19 goals in the 2017-18 Championship League?

    a. John Lundstram
    b. Clayton Donaldson
    c. Billy Sharp
    d. Leon Clarke

20. Jack Pickering scored 20 hat-tricks, the most in all competitions by a Sheffield United player.

    a. True
    b. False

QUIZ ANSWERS

1. C – Harry Johnson Jr.

2. B – False

3. A – Harry Hammond

4. A – Jimmy Dunne

5. D – 119

6. D – Arthur Brown

7. A – True

8. D – 15

9. B – James Beattie

10. A – Keith Edwards

11. C – Billy Sharp

12. A – True

13. B – 191

14. D – Neil Shipperley and Danny Webber

15. A – 35

16. A – True

17. C – Nick Blackman and Dave Kitson

18. D – 252

19. D – Leon Clarke

20. B – False

DID YOU KNOW?

1. The top scorers in Blades history are: Harry Johnson Jr., 252 (1916-31); Alan Woodward, 191 (1964-78); Doc Pace, 175 (1957-65); Keith Edwards, 171 (1976-86); Jimmy Dunne, 170 (1926-33); Jimmy Hagan, 151 (1938-57); Billy Gillespie, 137 (1911-31); Fred Tunstall, 135 (1920-32); Jock Dodds, 130 (1934–39); Brian Deane, 119 (1988-98); Jack Pickering, 119 (1927-48); Arthur Brown, 114 (1902-08); Alf Ringstead, 109 (1950-59); Billy Sharp, 103 (2004-present (as of June 2021)); Derek Hawksworth, 103 (1950-58); and Harold Brook, 101 (1940-54).

2. Of the 16 players who have scored 100 goals or more for the club, all played forward positions. All of them hailed from England except for Jimmy Dunne, Billy Gillespie, and Alf Ringstead, who were born in Ireland, and Jock Dodds, who hailed from Scotland. It should also be noted that Billy Sharp was still playing with the club in 2021 and climbing the scoring list.

3. The top scorer in Sheffield United history is Harry Johnson Jr with 252 goals in 395 games, including a club-record 201 league goals in 313 matches. The 5-foot-9-inch forward was born in Ecclesfield, Sheffield, and played for the local side beginning in 1916. He started at the age of 17 with the reserve team and ended up leading or sharing the team lead in scoring for nine straight seasons, from 1920-21 to

1928-29, peaking at 43 goals in 1927-28. Johnson helped the side win five Sheffield & Hallamshire County Cups and the FA Cup in 1924-25. He left for Mansfield Town and also leads that club in career goals, with 114. His father Harry and brother Tom also played for Sheffield United.

4. With 191 goals, Alan Woodward played 640 games for Sheffield United to rank second in all-time goals scored and third in appearances. The hometown player, nicknamed "Woody," made his debut in 1963-64 and remained with the club until 1978 when he headed to play in America. He was a dead-ball expert who sometimes scored directly from corner kicks. Woodward led the Blades in scoring in five seasons, including three in a row. He is the only Sheffield United player to be voted Player of the Year four times.

5. Derek "Doc" Pace joined the Blades on Boxing Day, December 26, 1957, from Aston Villa for a reported fee of £12,000, and he scored in his debut after just eight minutes the same day. He helped the side finish as the Second Division runner-up in 1960-61 and into the FA Cup semifinals, where he led the squad with 26 goals. In fact, Pace led the side in scoring for seven straight seasons, from 1957-58 to 1963-64, peaking at 33 goals in 1959-60. He was a fan favorite due to his enthusiasm, sportsmanship, shooting, and heading ability. Pace's last match for the team came in August 1964 before he joined Notts County. He scored 175 goals in just over 300 games for the Blades.

6. Winning the team's Player of the Year award for 1976-77 and 1983-84 was Keith Edwards, who notched 171 goals in 293 appearances for Sheffield United. He joined the club in 1975 and remained until leaving for Hull City in 1978. Edwards then returned for a second stint from 1981 to 1986, when he joined Leeds United. He led the team in scoring in 1976-77 and 1977-78 in his first spell and for all five seasons upon his return. He also led the Fourth Division in goals in 1981-82 and the Third Division in 1983-84. His best return came in 1983-84 when he netted 41 goals in all competitions. After retiring as a player, Edwards worked for BBC Radio Sheffield as a soccer commentator.

7. Born in Dublin, James "Jimmy" Dunne was a dual internationalist who played for two national Ireland teams. He also holds the record of consecutive goals scored at the elite level of English soccer, with tallies in 12 straight games in 1931-32. Dunne arrived at Sheffield United in 1926 from New Brighton and led the team in scoring for four straight seasons, from 1929-30 to 1932-33, with goal totals of 42, 50, 35, and 32, respectively. His 41 league goals in 1930-31 is a club record and represents the most goals scored by an Irish player in an English Football League campaign. The talented forward remained with the team until joining Arsenal in September 1933, after the Blades were relegated from the top-tier. Dunne scored an incredible 167 goals in 190 games for Sheffield United but sadly passed away at the age of 44 in 1949. His sons

Tommy and Jimmy and nephews Tommy Dunne and Christy Doyle were also pro soccer players.

8. England international Jimmy Hagan followed in his father Alf's footsteps and became a pro soccer player. Jimmy was a former England schoolboy player who joined Liverpool FC at the age of 15 in 1933. He joined Sheffield United from Derby County in November 1938 and scored in the final league game of the 1938-39 campaign to secure promotion from the Second Division to the top-tier as runner-up. Following World War II, Hagan initially refused to re-sign with the club but returned shortly into the 1946-47 campaign. The team was relegated in 1948-49, but Hagan helped it win the Second Division championship in 1952-53. The former skipper retired in 1958 after netting 151 goals and started his managerial career with Peterborough United before later managing in Portugal.

9. Billy Gillespie was an Irish international who began his career in Derry at the age of 17. He played with Leeds City from 1910 to 1912 before joining Sheffield United for a reported fee of £500, which was a Leeds record at the time. Gillespie was the Blades' captain from 1923 to 1930, and he led the team to its FA Cup triumph in 1924-25. He left the club in 1932 to become player-manager of Derry City after scoring 137 goals. He also tallied 13 goals in 25 matches with Ireland. Gillespie shared the scoring lead for Sheffield United in 1923-24 with Harry Johnson Jr. at 16

goals. He also helped the side win the 1914-15 FA Cup but was unable to play in the final.

10. English international Fred Tunstall was an outside-left who began his pro soccer career after the First World War, with Scunthorpe United. He then transferred to First Division Sheffield United in December 1920 for a reported £1,000 fee and went on to contribute 135 goals in just under 500 games. He helped the side win the FA Cup in 1924-25 by scoring the game-winner and tallied 20 goals in 1925-26 and 1927-28. Tunstall was also quite durable, as he missed fewer than 20 league games between 1921 and 1931. He left Bramall Lane in February 1933 for Halifax Town and later managed Boston United three different times.

CONCLUSION

You've just read over 125 years' worth of Sheffield United history in lighthearted, entertaining trivia quiz form. We hope the information has been educational, and we would be pleased if you've also stumbled upon something new along the way.

The Blades' story is certainly one worth telling because the team is one of the oldest and most famous in the UK. We hope all of your favorite club characters have been featured, but because Sheffield United was formed back in 1889, it was impossible to include everybody.

You now have 12 different trivia quiz chapters at your fingertips and a wide range of "Did You Know?" facts to prepare yourself to challenge and accept challenges from fellow Blades and soccer fans. You'll be able to solidly stand your ground as the most knowledgeable Sheffield United fan out there.

We've included dozens of informative and fun facts and trivia regarding the club's successes, disappointments, transfers, and records.

We hope you'll be inclined to share this trivia quiz book with others to help spread the word about the club's wonderful history to those who may not be fully aware of it.

There's still plenty of work ahead for Sheffield United as the club aims to soon become a permanent fixture in the Premier League and one day pack its bags for Europe.

Thank you kindly for being a loyal and passionate Sheffield United supporter and taking the time to read the latest Blades trivia publication.